# David

# Seeking God Faithfully

GENE A. GETZ

Foreword by Stephen F. Olford

Nashville, Tennessee

*Published by:*
*Broadman & Holman, Publishers*
*Nashville, Tennessee*

*Design:*
*Steven Boyd*

*4261-64*
*0-8054-6164-7*

*Dewey Decimal Classification: 248.842*
*Subject Heading: Men \ David \ Christian Life*
*Library of Congress Card Catalog Number: 94–40764*



***Library of Congress Cataloging-in-Publication Data***
*Getz, Gene A.*
*David: seeking God faithfully / Gene Getz.*
*p. cm. — (Men of character)*
*ISBN 0-8054-6164-7*
*1. David. (Biblical figure) 2. Bible. O.T. David—Criticism, interpretation, etc. I. Title. II. Series: Getz, Gene A. Men of character.*
*BS580.J7G47 1995*
*222'.2092—dc20*
*94-40764*
*CIP*

*6 7 8 9 10 04 03 02 01 00*

This book is affectionately dedicated to "a man after God's own heart"—Dr. Stephen Olford. Whether being taught by him or ministering with him, I'm always challenged to a deeper commitment to Jesus Christ. Thanks, dear friend, for being a godly mentor and model. You've touched my life and ministry deeply.

Other books in the *Men of Character* series:

- Elijah: Remaining Steadfast through Uncertainty
- Nehemiah: Becoming a Disciplined Leader
- Jacob: Following God without Looking Back
- Moses: Freeing Yourself to Know God
- Joshua: Living as a Consistent Role Model
- Joseph: Overcoming Obstacles through Faithfulness
- Abraham: Holding Fast to the Will of God
- Samuel: A Lifetime Serving God
- Daniel: Standing Firm for God
- The Apostles: Becoming Unified through Diversity

# *Contents*

# *Foreword*

David's name is mentioned more than one thousand times in the Bible—three times as often as Abraham and more times than Moses. What may really surprise you: David's name is recorded more often than the name of Jesus Christ. Indeed, our Lord is referred to in the Gospels as the "Son of David" at least twelve times.

Ask the average person what he remembers about David and he will probably recall his *greatest achievement* and his *greatest failure.* Who does not stand in awe of his great victory over the Philistine giant Goliath? And who can forget his greatest failure—his adulterous affair with Bathsheba? The first experience marks him as a Spirit-filled man who possessed great physical skill; the second exposes him as a lustful man who woefully deceived himself, rationalized his sin, and ended up committing murder. In a sense, the two events capture David's life. Because of his great heart, he often stood head and shoulders above his peers in doing great exploits for God. But because of his human weaknesses he sometimes found himself entangled in a web of sinful behavior.

David is well-known in history and in modern society. Christians have idealized him, Hollywood has exploited him, artists have sculpted him, and parents have named their sons after him. When my wife, Heather, gave birth to our firstborn we named him Jonathan ("given of God"). Then and there we decided that if the next arrival was a boy, his name would David ("beloved or dear"). Thank God, he has been just that as he has grown in grace and in the knowledge of our Lord and Savior Jesus Christ.

But how do we really know this man? What does the Bible actually say about him? What can we learn from David that will help us live more devoted lives for our Master and Friend, Jesus Christ? Who is this towering figure God describes as "a man after His own heart" (1 Sam. 13:14)?

My good friend and fellow pastor, Dr. Gene Getz, gives us the answers to these questions. Gene is a brilliant researcher. He did his doctoral work in this field, and his abilities are evident to all who read his books. As an expositor of God's Word, Gene's divinely endowed talents have been equally apparent as we have shared ministry together and as he has lectured at the Stephen Olford Center for Biblical Preaching in Memphis, Tennessee.

In this study on the life of David, Gene reveals the "inside story" of one of the most dominant characters of the Bible. His insights give us profound principles that apply to us *today.* Taking the principles seriously will help us all, by God's grace, to become men and women "after God's own heart."

Stephen F. Olford
Founder and Chairman of the Board
Stephen Olford Center for Biblical Preaching
Memphis, Tennessee

# Introduction

## *A Man Just Like Us*

David is one of my favorite Bible characters. It all began in Sunday School more than half a century ago. Who could forget reading about that great feat of valor—when a young shepherd boy, David, slew the giant Goliath with a single stone from his sling?

I now look at David through the eyes of an adult, and I see a man I really didn't know when I was a boy—a man whose failures were more enormous than his successes. Of course, as a youngster I couldn't have grasped how tragic David's decisions really were. His horrendous sins were beyond my ability to understand. Even now I sometimes wonder what really happened in David's heart and mind.

### A Man Who Admitted Failures

David is still one of my favorites—in spite of what I now know about his weaknesses. I still see a man whose heart was very soft and tender toward God. Though he became terribly self-deceived, even cruel and heartless—he mourned and wept over his sins when God put His finger of conviction on his soul. He was even willing to give his own life to stay God's hand of judgment on Israel, because he knew that he was really responsible for the nation's sinful actions (2 Sam. 24:17). This is what made him "a man after God's heart" until the day he died.

## A Man Who Experienced God's Grace

There's another reason I love the story of David. He illustrates how much God loves us all. When David should have died for his sins of adultery and murder, God responded to his repentant heart. He became a broken man.

How reassuring this is when I fail God! I know I serve a Father who is gracious and forgiving.

## A Man Who "Reaped What He Sowed"

I also love the story of David because he speaks so loudly to every man who faces the lure of the world, who is enticed by sin. His successes—but particularly his failures—send warnings that need to be heard. The message is loud and clear. It's the same message Paul outlined so succinctly centuries later in his letter to the Galatians: "Do not be deceived, God is not mocked; for whatever a man sows, this he will also reap. For the one who sows to his own flesh shall from the flesh reap corruption, but the one who sows to the Spirit shall from the Spirit reap eternal life" (Gal. 6:7–8).

## A Man after God's Own Heart

In spite of all of this, David remains one of the greatest men of the Bible. So join me in an exciting study—one that can touch your life deeply. I hope you'll never be the same again! If you've managed to escape David's sins, take heed! If you've fallen into the same pit, be encouraged! As long as you have breath, God is waiting to lift you out—even though you may face some difficult days because of your failures. As with David, God will never forsake you—no matter how far you stray from His perfect will.

Chapter 1

# *It's What's on the Inside that Counts*

Read 1 Samuel 9:1–16:23

One of the greatest challenges every Christian man faces is to keep his spiritual, ethical, and moral bearings on his journey through life. As I reflect on my own journey, I'm reminded of a number of close friends who once walked with God, particularly in their younger years. But at some point, they deliberately and willfully chose to walk out of the will of God. Though some enjoyed "the passing pleasures of sin" (Heb. 11:25), the ultimate results were tragic. Their marriages ended in divorce. Their children turned their anger against God. Their wives ended up in despair—or in their own moral failures. Some remarried and, sadly, some of those marriages also failed. Others failed in their business lives. Some died of sexually transmitted diseases—or committed suicide. In every instance, these men "reaped what they sowed."

## *A Familiar Scenario*

What I've just shared is not new. The Bible unfolds story after story of men who made a great start in life but ended in tragedy. We have, of course, plenty of positive examples—Abraham, Moses, Joshua, Nehemiah, Joseph, Elijah, Daniel, and many others. In fact, King David—the man we are about to get to know on a very intimate basis—was a "man after God's own heart." But he too failed God miserably at one point in his life. Though his heart was broken and he sincerely repented, he paid dearly in reaping what he sowed. Those who suffered the most from his sins were his own family members.

## *An Inseparable Relationship*

We cannot study the life of David without looking carefully at the life of Saul. These two men's lives are inseparably linked in the biblical narrative.

They have some things in common. Both were outstanding young men. Their early experiences with God reflected sincerity and humility. However, their great beginnings did not keep them from terrible failure later in life. The main difference: Once Saul turned away from God, he continued to deteriorate and his life ended in tragedy. David, however, sincerely sought God's forgiveness for his sins and returned to a vital relationship with God.

## *Looks Can Be Deceiving*

Saul's life pulsates with irony. Though "there was not a more handsome person than he among the sons of Israel," he became a weak and jealous man; though "from his shoulders and up he was taller" than all others (1 Sam. 9:2), on the inside he reflected a "smallness" of character that is shocking.

### A Sincere Beginning

The story of Saul's life is even more ironic when you study the unusual humility with which he began his career. When the prophet Samuel first approached Saul regarding his God-appointed post as the first king of Israel, Saul's response was definitely sincere: "Am I not a Benjamite, of the smallest of the tribes of Israel, and my family the least of all the families of the tribe of Benjamin?" (v. 21). When his appointed time came to be king, he disappeared. He literally hid from the leaders of Israel. When they eventually found him, they had to persuade him to accept the position (10:22–23).

## A Fall from Grace

This was Saul's early attitude and behavior. But once he became king, he failed miserably in doing the will of God. Often he took matters into his own hands. Once he impulsively usurped the priestly office by not waiting for Samuel to arrive to offer a sacrifice to God (13:12). And in the space of one chapter of the Bible, we see Saul flagrantly disobeying God (15:9), lying to cover up his sin (v. 13), and later rationalizing his behavior by putting the blame on others (vv. 20–21). Because of this tragic fall from grace, God rejected Saul as king (v. 28). Had he obeyed the Lord, he would have been blessed forever (13:13). But from this moment forward, his story is one of psychological, physical, and spiritual deterioration. He became a fearful, jealous, angry man. Dominated and controlled by his passions, his thinking became bizarre and confused, his actions immature and childish.

What makes this story even more tragic is that it was God Himself who chose and anointed Saul to be king over Israel (9:17; 10:1). To prepare him for this awesome responsibility, God actually "changed his heart" (10:9). We read that "the Spirit of the Lord" came upon him mightily. He prophesied along with the prophets of God (v. 6).

No man could have had a better start as a leader. But a great start—even with God's greatest blessing—does not guarantee a great ending. That's why Paul, reflecting on these Old Testament events in Israel's history, wrote these sobering words: "Therefore, let him who thinks he stands take heed lest he fall" (1 Cor. 10:12).

## A Staggering Judgment

Saul's sin and subsequent rejection by God initiated a search for a new king. Samuel, serving as God's prophetic voice, confronted Saul with a disquieting indictment and a staggering judgment: "But now your kingdom shall not endure. The LORD has sought out for Himself *a man after His own heart,* and the LORD has appointed him as ruler over His people, because you have not kept what the LORD commanded you" (1 Sam. 13:14).*

Saul's doom was sealed. Had he truly repented of his sins, there would have been no need for the tragic ending that characterized his final days. But his reign as king of Israel was destined for years of heartache and trouble, both for Saul and Israel. David was God's heir to the throne. In God's own time, this young man would replace Saul.

### Thirty-two Sad Years

Though God rejected Saul as king of Israel, He allowed him to rule for more than three decades (v. 1). But Saul did so without God's presence and power. As we'll see in the next chapter, God withdrew His Spirit from Saul and sent an evil spirit to trouble him.

## *Samuel's Grief*

The prophet Samuel, who had originally anointed Saul as king, experienced deep distress about Saul's disobedience and rejection. In fact, he was so grieved that he didn't "see Saul again until the day of his death" (15:35).

Samuel's grief is understandable. He was already "old and gray" when he anointed Saul as king (12:2). The prophet had great hopes for this brilliant and handsome young man, even though Samuel was displeased with Israel for asking for a king (8:6). Like an old pastor who had faithfully tended his flock, he was ready to turn the reins of leadership over to Saul, confident he would lead the sheep to even greener pastures.

---

* Hereafter, italicized words in Scripture quotations indicate the author's emphases.

But it didn't happen; Samuel's hopes were dashed. Saul, in spite of his great potential, deliberately walked out of God's will. He brought upon himself and the children of Israel some very serious consequences.

We all fail at times. Fortunately, most of our mistakes can be corrected. God in His grace enables us to forget the past, move on, and sometimes do even greater exploits for Him. But there are some sins with consequences that never can be rectified, particularly when they are committed by those in key leadership roles. King Saul had to face the consequences of his sins.

## *The Work of God Must Go On*

Disappointments in people must never thwart God's eternal purposes. This was the Lord's message to Samuel: "How long will you grieve over Saul, since I have rejected him from being king over Israel? Fill your horn with oil, and go; I will send you to Jesse the Bethlehemite, for I have selected a king for Myself among his sons" (16:1).

### Samuel's Fear

Samuel's grief blended with fear. He was afraid that King Saul would kill him if Saul discovered that he was searching for another leader. If Saul openly rebelled against God, he would certainly strike out at anyone who dared have a part in taking away his throne.

### Saul's Scapegoat

Since Samuel had faithfully served as the voice of God to Israel, he also had the responsibility to pronounce God's judgment upon Saul—a very difficult assignment (13:14). Consequently, the king turned his wrath on Samuel, plotting to kill him. Since he couldn't get his hands on God, he struck out at God's human mouthpiece. Samuel's grief focused not only on Saul's sad condition, but on the anger the king had turned on him. It was because of this fear that he "did not see Saul again until the day of his death" (15:35).

## Personal Reflections

I can identify with both of the reasons for Saul's grief. My experience as a pastor certainly does not match Samuel's in terms of both responsibility and emotion, but I *have* experienced the sadness that comes when someone I believe in walks out of the will of God. Furthermore, I know what it feels like to become the scapegoat for having to confront sin in another person's life. It's a painful experience—and one you never forget. It becomes particularly hurtful when the sinner "smoke screens" his own sins, makes himself the victim, and accuses the innocent party of his sinful behavior to get the attention off of himself. This is a common course of action by people who are confronted with their sins and who do not repent and humble themselves before God.

## *God's Cover*

In many respects, this was Samuel's predicament. He was a scapegoat for Saul's wrath. But God understood Samuel's feelings. He provided a protective cover—a spiritual context in which Samuel could carry out God's purposes without being discovered. He was to take a heifer to Bethlehem and offer a sacrifice to the Lord. This sincere worship experience also became a divine method for protecting Samuel from Saul.

## *A Twofold Purpose*

Samuel was obviously encouraged by God's instructions. He "did what the Lord said, and came to Bethlehem" (16:4). The elders of the city, when they saw Samuel approaching, were very fearful. They "came trembling to meet him and said, 'Do you come in peace?'" (v. 4).

You see, Samuel was well-known in Israel as the voice of God. Often he had to convey words of judgment because of Israel's sin. But not this time—he had come "in peace"; he'd come "to sacrifice to the Lord" (v. 5). But unknown to the people, God had two purposes in this sincere spiritual act of worship. Not only was it a divine "cover-up" to protect Samuel from Saul, but the sacrifice would become the means by which Samuel would select and anoint a new king over Israel.

## *Did Jesse Know?*

Did this aged father know what Samuel—and the Lord—had in mind? I believe he did. It seems only logical that these two men had met privately to discuss the ultimate purpose behind this rather unusual visit and sacrifice.

Imagine Jesse's excitement, mingled with fatherly pride, as he prepared to parade his sons before Samuel and God. David's conspicuous absence supports the theory that Jesse knew why Samuel had come. Would not God choose the son with the greatest physical stature and chronological maturity? After all, Saul was the tallest man in Israel. His replacement would surely need to be someone like him.

## *Samuel's Surprise*

When Jesse and his sons assembled for the sacrifice, Eliab—probably the tallest of the seven sons present—captured Samuel's attention immediately. "Surely the Lord's anointed is before Him," thought the old prophet (v. 6).

Wrong! God had another plan, and He made it clear to Samuel: "Do not look at his appearance or at the height of his stature, because I have rejected him; for God sees not as man sees, for man looks at the outward appearance, *but the Lord looks at the heart"* (v. 7).

God was looking for a man with character, a man whose heart was right toward Him. He was not interested in the size of the man, but rather in the "size" of his soul. As each of Jesse's sons paraded before Samuel, the Lord made it clear that His chosen vessel was not there. Puzzled, Samuel turned to Jesse and asked, "Are these all the children?" Jesse must have been surprised and skeptical. This is obvious in his response: "There remains yet the *youngest,* and behold, he is tending the sheep" (v. 11).

## *The Light Goes On*

Samuel refused to go ahead with the sacrifice until Jesse invited David. The moment this young man walked in, Samuel knew he was God's choice. He was a very handsome young man with red hair (he was ruddy) and soft eyes (v. 12). However, behind this external beauty was a heart that longed to know God.

One day, while tending his father's sheep, David composed some beautiful words as he led the flock through green pastures and by still pools of fresh water. As he faithfully protected them from wild animals in secluded valleys and poured oil on their wounds, David saw a parallel between himself and God, his divine Shepherd. Inspired both by his pastoral experience and the Holy Spirit, he wrote one of the most beautiful psalms ever created:

> The Lord is my shepherd, I shall not want.
>
> He makes me lie down in green pastures; He leads me beside quiet waters.
>
> He restores my soul; He guides me in the paths of righteousness for His name's sake.
>
> Even though I walk through the valley of the shadow of death, I fear no evil; for Thou art with me; Thy rod and Thy staff they comfort me.
>
> Thou dost prepare a table before me in the presence of my enemies; Thou hast anointed my head with oil; my cup overflows.
>
> Surely goodness and lovingkindness will follow me all the days of my life, and I will dwell in the house of the Lord forever. (Ps. 23)

## *Here Stood the Future King of Israel*

Standing before Samuel was God's choice—a man after His own heart. Since David had been faithful in small things, God would entrust him with greater things. He conscientiously took good care of Jesse's sheep, and God knew He could trust him with His own sheep—the children of Israel.

At that moment, God confirmed the choice: "Arise, anoint him; for this is he" (1 Sam. 16:12). Samuel, no doubt, breathed a sigh of relief and hastened to do what God had told him. As "Samuel took the horn of oil and anointed him in the midst of his brothers . . . the Spirit of the Lord came mightily upon David from that day forward" (v. 13).

## Becoming God's Man Today

*Principles to Live By*

### *Principle 1. We must constantly and consistently guard our hearts against deceitful influences, particularly as we grow older.*

Saul's fall from grace illustrates this lesson dramatically and convincingly. He began his career as a very humble and upright person. We've seen that God actually "changed his heart" in order to prepare him for kingship (10:9). But prominence and success soon went to his *head,* which always affects the *heart*—the area where we are all vulnerable. Saul's sinful nature took over and soon dominated his total being—and his actions. Self-centeredness became a way of life.

David illustrates this lesson positively. He was a man after *God's* heart. He desired to do the will of God, which is beautifully illustrated in another one of his psalms: "Who may ascend into the hill of the Lord? And who may stand in His holy place? He who has clean hands and a pure *heart,* who has not lifted up his soul to falsehood, and has not sworn deceitfully. He shall receive a blessing from the Lord and righteousness from the God of his salvation"(Ps. 24:3–5).

### *Don't Misunderstand*

Saul was not all bad and David all good. They both were human beings with human weaknesses. The difference lay in their life focus. They both had the same potential. But Saul more and more followed his selfish, egocentric desires. David, especially in his early life, earnestly followed God's ways. In his later years—even when he failed God miserably—he always turned back to the Lord.

### *False Motives*

It's true that Saul confessed his sins (1 Sam. 15:24). But his repentance was manipulative and superficial. Because God sees the heart, He did not respond to Saul.

I believe that Saul truly wanted to be forgiven. But his confession was based on false motives. He felt sorry because he got caught! He believed confession was his only chance to maintain his kingship.

### *It Happens Today*

I'm reminded of a man who had fallen into deep sin. When his web of deceit and immorality was discovered, he fell to his knees and sobbed uncontrollably, seeking forgiveness and mercy. Everyone—including his wife—felt his confession was sincere.

Sadly, we were wrong! Shortly after this man sought public forgiveness, he continued to lie and deceive.

Men who get caught—like Saul—often feel sorry because they've been caught, not because they've wounded the heart of God.

### *Let Us Judge Ourselves*

I share this story not to judge this person but to help us judge ourselves. Many Christians have been sidetracked by not guarding their hearts. Any one of us can go astray! Jeremiah warned against this problem when he wrote, "The heart is more deceitful than all else and is desperately sick" (Jer. 17:9).

Solomon also wrote, "Watch over your heart with all diligence, for from it flow the springs of life" (Prov. 4:23).

### *Principle 2. We are often vulnerable to pride and arrogance when we have a weak self-image and feel insecure about who we really are.*

Ironically, men who are insecure and fearful are often the most vulnerable to pride and arrogance when they are placed in positions of power. What appeared to be true meekness and humility turn out to be a sense of worthlessness.

I once knew a man who fits this description. In many respects he was brilliant. But he had some serious personality flaws. When challenged, he became threatened—and angry. When successful, he fought pride.

Life was not easy for this man. Unfortunately, he also made life very difficult for those who worked closely with him and he often embarrassed his supervisors. Sadly, rather than being removed from his job or transferred to a more suitable position, he was promoted—and that made his problems even worse.

Was this part of Saul's problem? After all, when he was to be anointed king, he ran to hide. Was this true humility—or insecurity?

Only God knows Saul's heart. After all, God chose him and anointed him. If indeed he was suffering from a poor self-image in spite of his size and good looks, God wanted to help Saul overcome the problem and be successful. Consequently, He empowered Saul with His Holy Spirit.

However, some people cannot handle spiritual power either. It only accentuates their tendency toward pride. They use their spiritual influence to build themselves up and to control others.

Whether or not this was true of Saul is speculative. However, the principle is still true: We often succumb to pride and arrogance when we have a weak self-image and feel insecure. We often can't handle success and prominence—even if it's a spiritual position and God has put us here. If this is true, we should admit our problems to some close Christian brothers, seek their prayers and be accountable to them. At the same time, we should double our efforts to guard against Satan's efforts to trip us!

### *Principle 3. We must be careful when we select leaders. External appearances can deceive.*

Saul won respect because of his stature and other physical attributes. But his heart, though initially humble, was subject to deceitful influences. David also possessed many external attributes, but he was a man of different internal qualities.

#### *Churches Select Leaders*

Today, we have to make many "people choices." Churches must select deacons, elders, teachers, pastors, and other leaders. People who are not qualified can destroy God's work. This is why Paul specified very clearly the qualities for church leadership (1 Tim. 3; Titus 1).[1]

#### *We Choose Marriage Partners*

Men choose women to be their wives. Women choose men to be their husbands. Outward beauty and external appearances do not make a marriage endure. Yet many of us look first at these superficial qualities. When choosing a wife (or husband), remember: It's the heart that reflects depth or superficiality. A mate whose heart is sensitive toward God has a heart that also will be sensitive toward you.

#### *Businessmen Choose Associates*

Businessmen, too, choose associates and employees. When making any of these choices, it's important to consider God's words to Samuel: "God sees not as man sees, for man looks at the outward appearance, but the Lord looks at the heart" (1 Sam. 16:7). Our goal in all of our people choices should be to develop God's perspective.

*We All Choose Friends*

People choices affect us all since we all select friends. The Scriptures teach that bad company can corrupt any of us and lead us down a wrong path. We tend to imitate the bad qualities in our friends rather than our friends imitating our good attributes.

Paul warned the Corinthians of this when he wrote, "Do not be bound together with unbelievers; for what partnership have righteousness and lawlessness, or what fellowship has light with darkness? Or what harmony has Christ with Belial, or what has a believer in common with an unbeliever?" (2 Cor. 6:14–15).

Paul, of course, was not telling us that it is wrong to associate with people who are unbelievers. This would be impossible since we "would have to go out of the world" (1 Cor. 5:10). What Paul *was* saying is that we cannot associate with sinful people on a deep friendship or close associate level without endangering our own spiritual lives. We certainly can witness to these people, but we cannot have deep relationships with them. Consequently, we must select our friends carefully.

## Becoming a Man after God's Heart

*A Decision That Changes Lives Forever*

Remember, before you can put into practice these three lessons, you must have a renewed heart. Paul makes clear how this can happen: "If you confess with your mouth, 'Jesus as Lord,' and believe in your heart that God raised him from the dead, you will be saved. For it is with your heart that you believe and are justified, and it is with your mouth that you confess and are saved" (Rom. 10:9,10, NIV).

Have you taken this step of faith? If you receive Jesus Christ as your personal Lord and Savior, God will change your heart and give you new life in Christ. This decision will change your life forever.

### *Are You a Man after God's Heart?*

As you evaluate the following principles, pray and ask the Holy Spirit to impress on your heart one lesson you need to apply more effectively in your life. Then write out a specific goal. For example, you may be vulnerable to pride and arrogance because you have a weak self-image and feel insecure about who you really are. You may cover up your insecurity by giving the impression you're really in control.

Here, once again, are the principles:

- ➢ We must constantly and consistently guard our hearts against deceitful influences, particularly as we grow older.
- ➢ We are often vulnerable to pride and arrogance when we have a weak self-image and feel insecure about who we really are.
- ➢ We must be careful when we select people for significant leadership roles. External appearances can be deceiving.

### *Set a Goal*

With God's help, I will begin immediately to carry out the following goal in my life:

________________________________________

________________________________________

________________________________________

________________________________________

### *Memorize the Following Scripture*

*I have been crucified with Christ; and it is no longer I who live, but Christ lives in me; and the life which I now live in the flesh I live by faith in the Son of God, who loved me, and delivered Himself up for me.*

GALATIANS 2:20

Chapter 2

# *A Penetrating Look at a Man's Heart*

Read Psalms 8; 9; 14; 15; 19; 26; 29; 36; 37; 40; 51; 61; 65; 86; 131; 138; 139

We live in a world obsessed with externals. Visit any health club. Wall-to-wall mirrors reflect people looking at themselves as they pump iron. Stop for a moment and watch people watch themselves.

As a man, stand on the street corner and watch your own species. When a beautiful woman walks by (I'm sure you'll notice her), note the men who watch her coming, who follow her with their eyes—and watch some who actually stop in their tracks and turn completely around as she passes by. What a reflection! An embarrassing one—because they're probably mirroring our own hearts!

Glance at the number of exercise videos paraded on the market. You can see everything from Jane Fonda's routines to an increasing number of not-so-famous gurus promising to enhance your physical appearance.

Watch the ads on television—from cosmetics to clothes. Most have one message: make yourself look better, more attractive, more beautiful. Develop your sex appeal!

We do focus on externals. We're obsessed. Interestingly, God says "for man looks at the *outward appearance,* but the Lord looks at the *heart*" (1 Sam. 16:7).

This does not mean we shouldn't look the best we can. But to focus on externals is to overlook the real criteria for determining what a person is like.

Externally, Saul was a stunning and startling specimen of humanity. But his heart revealed a man with serious spiritual weaknesses. David also was a good-looking lad, but more importantly, he had a heart that loved God.

## *God's Criteria*

When Samuel pronounced God's judgment on Saul, he stated that "the Lord has sought out for Himself a man after His own *heart"* (13:14). More specifically, Samuel was saying that Saul was not a man after God's heart. David was!

Later, when Samuel was looking for Saul's replacement among the sons of Jesse, God made it very clear that the new king was to be chosen—not on the basis of external appearances, but on the basis of internal qualities: "For God sees not as man sees, for man looks at the outward appearance, but the LORD looks at the heart" (16:7).

## *What Is the Heart?*

In both the Old and New Testaments, the word *heart* refers to the center of an individual's mental, emotional, and spiritual life. It's the "innermost part of man." The heart reflects the real person.

- As the *mental center,* the heart knows, understands, reflects, considers, and remembers.

- As the *emotional center,* it is the seat of joy, courage, pain, anxiety, despair, sorrow, and fear.

- As the *moral center,* God "tries the *heart,*" "sees the *heart,*" "refines the *heart,*" and "searches the *heart.*"

The Scriptures indicate that a person may have an "evil *heart,*" be "godless in *heart,*" be "perverse and deceitful in *heart,*" and "harden his *heart.*" But a person also can have a "clean *heart*" and a "new *heart.*"[1]

## *David's Reflections*

To understand David's heart, there are two crucial questions that we can ask and answer from reading his own Scriptural writings:

- What was David's view of God?
- What was God's view of David?

David's psalms give us a rich source in which to answer these questions. Most scholars believe David wrote at least seventy-three of these beautiful literary pieces. They communicate clearly David's view of God and God's view of David.[2]

## *David's View of God*

Every psalm David wrote gives us fascinating insights into his ideas, attitudes, and feelings toward God. Following are some selective highlights that focus on David's references to "the *heart.*"

### The Omnipotent Creator

*"The heavens are telling."* Several of David's psalms focus on God's creative power. David was an outdoorsman, a man who spent many hours—day and night—absorbing the splendor, beauty, and mysteries of nature. Inspired by God's Spirit, he expressed his thoughts in poetry. Psalm 19, for example, reveals David's convictions and feelings about the firmament, particularly the sun in its journey across space:

> The heavens are telling of the glory of God;
> And the firmament is declaring the work
> of His hands.

Day to day pours forth speech,
And night to night reveals knowledge.
There is no speech, nor are there words;
Their voice is not heard.
Their line has gone out through all the earth,
And their utterances to the end of the world.
In them He has placed a tent for the sun,
Which is as a bridegroom coming out
of his chamber;
It rejoices as a strong man to run his course.
Its rising is from one end of the heavens,
And its circuit to the other end of them;
And there is nothing hidden from its heat. (19:1–6)

*"The Voice of the LORD."* David's view of God's creative power in nature often generated praise, thanksgiving and worship in his heart. In Psalm 29 he writes about a storm. While most of us understandably focus on our fears and anxieties in the midst of this kind of natural turbulence, David's heart focused on God. Though he too probably experienced fear, what he observed and felt reflected the "voice of the LORD":

The voice of the LORD is upon the waters;
The God of glory thunders,
The LORD is over many waters.
The voice of the LORD is powerful,
The voice of the LORD is majestic.
The voice of the LORD breaks the cedars;
Yes, the LORD breaks in pieces
the cedars of Lebanon.
And He makes Lebanon skip like a calf,
And Sirion like a young wild ox.
The voice of the LORD hews out flames of fire.
The voice of the LORD shakes the wilderness;
The LORD shakes the wilderness of Kadesh.
The voice of the LORD makes the deer to calve,

And strips the forests bare,
And in His temple everything says, 'Glory!' (29:3–9)

*"They shout for joy!"* David also was impressed with the four seasons—and God's provisions to cause the earth to produce all kinds of vegetation to sustain both mankind and animals. Note Psalm 65:9–13:

> Thou dost visit the earth, and cause it to overflow;
> Thou dost greatly enrich it;
> The stream of God is full of water;
> Thou dost prepare their grain, for thus Thou dost
>     prepare the earth.
> Thou dost water its furrows abundantly;
> Thou dost settle its ridges;
> Thou dost soften it with showers;
> Thou dost bless its growth.
> Thou hast crowned the year with Thy bounty,
> And Thy paths drip with fatness.
> The pastures of the wilderness drip,
> And the hills gird themselves with rejoicing.
> The meadows are clothed with flocks,
> And the valleys are covered with grain;
> They shout for joy, yes, they sing.

## The Omniscient God

*"Such knowledge is too wonderful for me!"* David understood that God knew *everything* about him—every detail of his heart and his actions—at any given moment. This is apparent in the opening verses of Psalm 139:

> O LORD, Thou hast searched me and known me.
> Thou dost know when I sit down and when I rise up;
> Thou dost understand my thought from afar.
> Thou dost scrutinize my path and my lying down,
> And art intimately acquainted with all my ways.

Even before there is a word on my tongue,
Behold, O LORD, Thou dost know it all.
Thou hast enclosed me behind and before,
And laid Thy hand upon me.
Such knowledge is too wonderful for me;
It is too high, I cannot attain to it. (vv.1–6)

## The Omnipresent Spirit

*"Where can I flee from Thy presence?"* David not only viewed God as omnipotent (all-powerful) and omniscient (all-knowing), but also as omnipresent. In other words, God was everywhere David went—to guide him, to protect him, to comfort him, and to search out his heart:

Where can I go from Thy Spirit?
Or where can I flee from Thy presence?
If I ascend to heaven, Thou art there;
If I make my bed in Sheol, behold, Thou art there.
If I take the wings of the dawn,
If I dwell in the remotest part of the sea,
Even there Thy hand will lead me,
And Thy right hand will lay hold of me.
If I say, "Surely the darkness will overwhelm me,
And the light around me will be night,"
Even the darkness is not dark to Thee,
And the night is as bright as the day.
Darkness and light are alike to Thee. (139:7–12)

## The God of Loving Concern

*"What is man, that Thou dost take thought of him?"* If God was so involved in preserving what He had created in nature, how much more was He concerned for all mankind? David understood this great truth. Furthermore, the fact that the Lord gave human beings a certain degree of authority and control over His natural creation overwhelmed David, as he expressed in Psalm 8:

> When I consider Thy heavens,
> the work of Thy fingers,
> The moon and the stars, which Thou hast ordained;
> What is man, that Thou dost take thought of him?
> And the son of man, that Thou dost care for him?
> Yet Thou hast made him a little lower than God,
> And dost crown him with glory and majesty!
> Thou dost make him to rule over the works of Thy hands;
> Thou hast put all things under his feet,
> All sheep and oxen,
> And also the beasts of the field,
> The birds of the heavens, and the fish of the sea,
> Whatever passes through the paths of the seas.
> "O LORD, our Lord,
> How majestic is Thy name in all the earth!". (vv. 3–9)

## The God of Lovingkindness

*"Thy Lovingkindness . . . Thy Faithfulness . . . Thy Righteousness."* The vastness of the universe also reminded David of God's personal attributes. Note Psalm 36:5–6:

> Thy lovingkindness, O LORD,
> extends to the heavens,
> Thy faithfulness reaches to the skies.
> Thy righteousness is like the mountains of God;
> Thy judgments are like a great deep.

Many other psalms reveal David's view of God. But these few demonstrate dramatically why David was "a man after God's heart."

## *God's View of David*

How did God view David? When the Lord looked beyond this young man's outward appearance and into his heart, what did He see? Again, David's psalms give us a significant profile of his inner qualities. These were not just verbalizations but expressions of his heart.

## A Believing Heart

*"A fool has said . . . 'There is no God.'"* When God looked at David's heart He saw a man who believed in His existence. So convinced was David of this existence that He wrote: "The fool has said in his *heart,* 'There is no God'" (Ps. 14:1; 53:1).

The point is clear! When God looked at David's heart the day Samuel chose him to be king, He saw a heart that believed in His eternal being. To David, any man who denied the reality of God was a fool.

## A Thankful Heart

*"I will give thanks!"* God also saw a thankful heart—a heart totally overwhelmed by God's love and provision. This is reflected in a number of psalms David wrote:

> I will *give thanks* to the LORD with all my *heart;*
> I will tell of all Thy wonders.
> I will be glad and exult in Thee;
> I will sing praise to Thy name, O Most High. (9:1–2)
>
> Teach me Thy way, O LORD; I will walk in Thy truth;
> Unite my *heart* to fear Thy name.
> I will *give thanks* to Thee, O Lord my God, with all my
> *heart,*
> And will glorify Thy name forever. (86:11–12)
>
> I will *give Thee thanks* with all my *heart;*
> I will sing praises to Thee before the gods.
> I will bow down toward Thy holy temple,
> And *give thanks* to Thy name
> for Thy lovingkindness and Thy truth;
> For Thou hast magnified Thy word according
> to all Thy name. (138:1–2)

## A Truthful Heart

*"He Who . . . Speaks Truth in His Heart."* David's view of God caused him to want to reflect God's character. This is very apparent in Psalm 15:

O LORD, who may abide in Thy tent?
Who may dwell on Thy holy hill?
He who walks with integrity,
and works righteousness,
And speaks truth in his *heart.*
He does not slander with his tongue,
Nor does evil to his neighbor,
Nor takes up a reproach against his friend. (vv. 1–3)

## An Open Heart

*"Know My Heart."* David knew God was omniscient. He didn't try to hide from the all-knowing Creator. His heart was open and transparent:

Examine me, O LORD, and try me;
Test my mind and my *heart.* (26:2)

Search me, O God, and know my *heart;*
Try me and know my anxious thoughts;
And see if there be any hurtful way in me,
And lead me in the everlasting way. (139:23–24)

## An Expectant Heart

*"The Desires of Your Heart."* David trusted God to meet his needs:

Delight yourself in the Lord;
And He will give you the desires of your *heart.*
Commit your way to the LORD,
Trust also in Him, and He will do it. (37:4–5)

## A Heart That Remembered God's Law

*"The Meditation of My Heart."* Because David wanted to do God's will in all things, he committed the law of God to memory. He wrote: "I delight to do Thy will, O my God; Thy Law is within my *heart"* (Ps. 40:8).

Psalm 19 reflects even more graphically David's attitude toward God's Word:

The judgments of the LORD are true; they are righteous
altogether.
They are more desirable than gold, yes, than much fine
gold;
Sweeter also than honey and the drippings of the
honeycomb.
Moreover, by them Thy servant is warned;
In keeping them there is great reward. (19:9–11)

David beautifully culminated his concern about doing the will of God with this prayer:

Let the words of my mouth and the meditation of my
*heart*
Be acceptable in Thy sight,
O LORD, my rock and my redeemer. (19:14)

## A Sorrowful Heart

*"A Contrite Heart."* When David sinned against God, he demonstrated true remorse. Unlike Saul, who sought forgiveness because he had been caught and feared losing his position, David sought forgiveness because he had failed the God he loved. Psalm 51 is one of his best-known poetic expressions—a prayer every man who wants to be godly should pray on a regular basis:

Create in me a clean *heart,* O God,
And renew a steadfast spirit within me. . .
The sacrifices of God are a broken spirit;
A broken and a contrite *heart,* O God, Thou wilt not
despise. (51:10, 17)

## A Humble Heart

*"My Heart Is Not Proud."* David knew his limitations. His view of himself was seen against his view of God's greatness. He knew he had strengths, but also great weaknesses.

When God looked upon David's heart, He saw a man

with a proper balance in the area of self-image. This is reflected in one of David's shortest psalms:

> O LORD, my *heart* is not proud, or my eyes haughty;
> Nor do I involve myself in great matters,
> Or in things too difficult for me. (131:1)

## A Dependent Heart

*"When My Heart Is Faint."* David knew how much he needed God to sustain him. He could not fulfill his responsibilities in his own strength. Note Psalm 61:

> Hear my cry, O God;
> Give heed to my prayer.
> From the end of the earth I call to Thee, when my *heart* is faint;
> Lead me to the rock that is higher than I.
> For Thou hast been a refuge for me,
> A tower of strength against the enemy.
> Let me dwell in Thy tent forever;
> Let me take refuge in the shelter of Thy wings. (vv. 1-4)

## *A Man in God's Mirror*

When God looked at David that day he was anointed king, He saw a man after His own heart—a man who understood who He really is. David was deeply affected by the reality of God's omnipotence, His omniscience, His omnipresence, His lovingkindness, faithfulness and righteousness.

God also saw a man who was personally affected by his perceptions of the Lord of the universe. Looking beyond David's attractive red hair, beautiful eyes and handsome appearance, the Lord saw a man with a believing heart, a thankful heart, a truthful heart, an open heart, an expectant heart, a heart that cherished God's law, a sorrowful heart, a humble and dependent heart. This is why God chose David to be the future king of Israel.

## Becoming God's Man Today

*Principles to Live By*

David was not a perfect man. But he had a proper view of God, which affected his own heart and caused him to be a person God could use, in spite of his human weaknesses.

What about you? What is your view of God? And what is His view of you? When you think about God, what goes through your mind and your emotions? When God looks beyond your external appearance, what does He see?

### *Principle 1. David's view of God should be our view of God.*

The following questions will help you evaluate your view of God:

1. When I think of God's omnipotence (that He is all-powerful), how does it affect my life? How should it affect my life?
2. When I think of God's omniscience (that He knows everything), how does it affect my life? How should it affect my life?
3. When I think of God's omnipresence (that He is present everywhere), how does it affect my life? How should it affect my life?
4. When I think of God's loving concern for all men (and for me personally), how does it affect my life? How should it affect my life?
5. When I think of God's faithfulness, how does it affect my life? How should it affect my life?
6. When I think of God's lovingkindness, righteousness, and holiness, how does it affect my life? How should it affect my life?

### *Principle 2. God's view of David should be His view of us.*

Using David's example, evaluate your own heart attitudes. On the following checklist, rate your personal "heart health" with the following numbers:

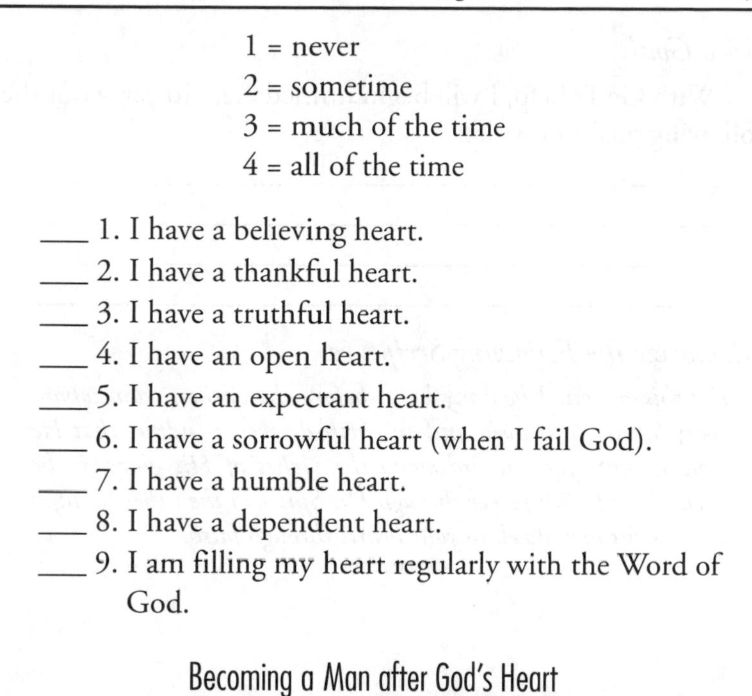

1 = never
2 = sometime
3 = much of the time
4 = all of the time

___ 1. I have a believing heart.
___ 2. I have a thankful heart.
___ 3. I have a truthful heart.
___ 4. I have an open heart.
___ 5. I have an expectant heart.
___ 6. I have a sorrowful heart (when I fail God).
___ 7. I have a humble heart.
___ 8. I have a dependent heart.
___ 9. I am filling my heart regularly with the Word of God.

## Becoming a Man after God's Heart

The above exercise will help you pinpoint the areas in your life where you need to improve your view of God and the way God views you. Select those areas where you check a "1 = never" and a "2 = sometime" and determine—with God's help—to become a man after God's heart.

*Warning*

Don't be discouraged. God is in the business of changing human hearts.

*Remember:*

He is the omnipotent, omniscient, and omnipresent God. If He can control the universe, He can control your life—if you'll let Him. The process, however, must begin with you, your will, your desire to have Him change you. God will not force Himself on you. But if you take a step toward Him, He will take a step toward you. This is what James said when he wrote, *"Draw near to God and He will draw near to you"* (James 4:8).

## *Set a Goal*

With God's help, I will begin immediately to carry out the following goal in my life:

____________________________________________

____________________________________________

____________________________________________

____________________________________________

## *Memorize the Following Scripture*

*For this reason, I bow my knees before the Father, from whom every family in heaven and on earth derives its name, that He would grant you, according to the riches of His glory, to be strengthened with power through His Spirit in the inner man; so that Christ may dwell in your hearts through faith.*

Ephesians 3:14–17a

Chapter 3

# *An Unforgettable Contrast*

Read 1 Samuel 16:1–23

Life is filled with contrasts. Some are good and some are bad—a contrast in itself. Some happen quickly, such as a tranquil environment suddenly rocked by an earthquake. Some happen gradually, as when the sun sets transforming our part of the earth from light to darkness. Some are concurrent experiences, such as sitting down to a meal with "sweet and sour" flavors mixed together.

All of these events become metaphors when describing personal experiences—such as sudden life-and-death catastrophes. Most of us have witnessed illnesses that slowly take their toll and eventually leave strong, healthy people weak and sickly,—or the mixture of joy and pain in childbirth.

Contrasts and incongruities are a part of life. That's why we have used contrast as a literary technique ever since we began expressing reality—as well as fiction—in writing. Contrasts get our attention!

Biblical writers, inspired by the Holy Spirit, also used this literary technique. The author of 1 Samuel used a startling contrast that should turn our heads every time we read it. It presents opposites we'll never forget. When Samuel anointed David to be the second king of Israel, we read back-to-back statements that are startling:

- "The Spirit of the Lord came mightily upon David" (16:13).

- "Now the Spirit of the Lord departed from Saul" (v. 14).

## *The Holy Spirit and Old Testament Leaders*

There are a number of examples in the Old Testament of the Spirit of God coming upon men. God sovereignly selected them for special tasks, and they often were able to prophesy and speak God's Word to the children of Israel.

### Architectural Skills Without Training

The Lord selected Bezalel to take responsibility to build the Tabernacle in the wilderness. To help him achieve this incredible feat, the Lord anointed Bezalel in a special way with His Spirit. Communicating directly with Moses, God said, "*I have filled him with the Spirit of God* in wisdom, in understanding, in knowledge, and in all kinds of craftsmanship, to make artistic designs for work in gold, in silver, and in bronze, and in the cutting of stones for settings, and in the carving of wood, that he may work in all kinds of craftsmanship" (Exod. 31:3–5).

God sovereignly gave "spiritual gifts" to achieve His divine purposes in Israel and in the world.

### Moses and His Seventy Associates

Moses also experienced God's special anointing. But at one time when he was terribly discouraged with what appeared to be an impossible task, God also anointed seventy other men to help him lead the children of Israel through the wilderness:

> The Lord therefore said to Moses, 'Gather for Me seventy men from the elders of Israel, whom you know to be the elders of the people and their officers and bring them to the tent of

> meeting, and let them take their stand there with you. Then I will come down and speak with you there, and I will *take of the Spirit who is upon you, and will put Him upon them*; and they shall bear the burden of the people with you, so that you shall not bear it all alone.'" (Num. 11:16–17)

## More Outstanding Examples

We can find a number of other illustrations of this Old Testament phenomenon:

- ➢ Balaam (Num. 24:2)
- ➢ Joshua (Num. 27:18; Deut. 34:9)
- ➢ Othniel (Judg. 3:10)
- ➢ Gideon (Judg. 6:34)
- ➢ Jephthah (Judg. 11:29)
- ➢ Samson (Judg. 14:6,19; 15:14)

In each instance, the Spirit of the Lord came upon these men, giving them supernatural abilities.

This also happened to Saul when God chose him to be the first king of Israel. We read that "God changed his heart. . . . and *the Spirit of God came upon him mightily*" (1 Sam. 10:9–10), just as the Spirit came upon David the day he also was anointed to be Saul's replacement. This was not just an experience for men. Miriam, Moses' sister, is identified as a "prophetess" (Exod. 15:20), as well as Deborah who served as a judge in Israel (Judg. 4:4).

# *A Tragic Decline*

Saul's life declined tragically when the Spirit came upon David—but departed from Saul.

Seldom do we read in the Old Testament that God—after anointing a person in a special way with His Spirit—deliberately withdrew His Presence. True, His Spirit's influence in certain gifted men was more obvious at certain times, as in Samson's life. But in between such unusual manifestations, the Spirit evidently did not depart from these men as He did from Saul—even when they were living carnal and sinful lives.[1]

When David fell from grace, he was terribly afraid that he might lose God's Spirit because of his sins. He certainly had not forgotten what happened to Saul. It had been indelibly impressed on his young mind. Consequently, when he failed God he prayed that the Lord would not take His Holy Spirit from him (Ps. 51:11). Because of David's sincere repentance and godly sorrow—reflected in the total context of Psalm 51—it evidently never happened.

## To Whom God Gives Much, He Expects Much!

Jesus stated this principle very clearly in one of His parables (Luke 12:42–48).

Saul *had* been given much. God's Spirit came mightily upon him. And in the full light of the Lord's special grace, he deliberately disobeyed and refused to sincerely acknowledge his sin. Rather, he hardened his heart.

Saul *did* lose the Holy Spirit! He was persistently disobedient. When Samuel confronted him, he defended his behavior with rationalizations and dishonest excuses. When he discovered he could not manipulate the Lord, he hardened his heart even more.

## Going from Bad to Worse

Unfortunately, one step backward in rebellion towards God often leads to another. Once the "Spirit of the LORD departed from Saul . . . an evil spirit from the LORD terrorized him" (1 Sam. 16:14).

This was an unusual event in Old Testament history, and it calls for some careful thought. What actually happened to make this startling contrast even more profound? There are two main opinions among Bible scholars.

## Was This a Demon?

Some believe this was indeed an evil spirit—a demonic presence. Saul's symptoms reflect what might be interpreted as psychological disturbance, but some believe the direct cause was an outside force that had access to his inner being. Though he suffered great periods of neurotic anxiety and emotional stress, alternating between deep depression and fits of rage, they conclude the root cause was demonic—not merely psychological.

## Did Saul Dabble in the Occult?

If this interpretation is correct, once God's Spirit departed from Saul, he may have engaged in occult practices that were very prevalent in the pagan world. Aware that his supernatural abilities from God had been taken away, it would be only natural for a man like Saul—in his insecurity and anger—to reach out to whatever "source" he could to regain his personal power.

We must understand that Satan and his cohorts are a powerful and evil force that is nearer to every one of us than we often realize. The apostle Paul taught about this reality when he wrote to the Ephesian Christians that their struggle was "not against flesh and blood, but against the rulers, against the authorities, against the powers of this dark world and against the spiritual forces of evil in the heavenly realms" (Eph. 6:12, NIV). King Saul may have turned to these "forces of evil" once the Lord's Spirit left him.

## A Puzzling Question

If the "evil spirit" troubling Saul was a demon, how do we explain that it came "from the Lord"? Does this mean that God *permitted* the spirit to come upon Saul since He is sovereign over all things? Though God has given Satan and his company of evil spirits a great deal of freedom, they cannot do anything without His approval, especially in the lives of His children (see Job 1–2).

## Was Saul a True Believer?

It's my personal opinion that Saul was one of God's true children. Disobedient, yes! But he was a child of God nevertheless. When the Lord took His Holy Spirit from him, I do not believe He took away his salvation. As a free moral agent, Saul had the liberty to turn away from God and dabble in the world of evil. If he did take this step, he was experiencing the terrible consequences. He was caught in the clutches of an evil spirit.

I can accept this interpretation as valid, especially since Saul in his final days participated in a seance (1 Sam. 28:7). However, I prefer another opinion.

## Was This a Unique Psychological Condition?

The word "evil" in 1 Samuel 16:14 can refer to discontent, calamity, or disaster. In this case, the Lord could have sent to Saul this kind of "spirit" or sense of distress and anxiety. Rather than being an outside evil force, such as a demon, the "spirit" could have been a psychological condition within Saul's inner being which resulted directly from God's judgment.

If this is true, Saul's case was different from ordinary demon possession and very different from a typical psychological problem. The emotional turmoil would have come directly from God because of Saul's persistent disobedience. Though Satan certainly would have been involved in tormenting Saul, it would not have been an evil spirit per se that was troubling him.

Whatever position we take in explaining what happened to Saul, one thing's for sure: Saul brought this condition on himself! It began when he deliberately disobeyed God's personal and direct communication with him. And once God's Spirit left him, Saul deteriorated in his relationship both with God and people. He could have thrown himself upon God's mercy to deliver him from this miserable state, but he chose to try to solve the problem in his own strength.

## *Once Again, God's Grace*

Much of the story of David's life also is the story of God's grace toward Saul. In fact, God's judgment was discipline—an act of love designed to turn Saul's heart back toward righteousness.

In many respects, Saul represents the Christian in rebellion against God. On the other hand, David's involvement in Saul's life reflects God's love through Jesus Christ.

Saul's servants recognized his problem immediately. They suggested finding someone who could play quiet and melodic music, specifically on a harp (v. 16), to calm him.

Saul responded positively to their suggestion (v. 17). Providentially, one of Saul's servants had become acquainted with David and knew this young shepherd boy not only was "a mighty man of valor, a warrior, one prudent in speech, and a handsome man," but also a "skillful musician" (v. 18). The servant also knew that "the Lord was with David." He was obviously aware that the Holy Spirit had empowered David with supernatural wisdom and skill.

### God's Providential Care

These events did not happen by chance. Rather, David—the man who eventually would replace Saul—became the means whereby Saul could find relief from the "spirit" troubling him. Furthermore, I believe God was giving Saul an opportunity to learn firsthand from David what kind of man He honors. Since Saul would not listen to Samuel, God—in His grace—showed him David.

David experienced immediate rapport with the king of Israel. Saul "loved him greatly" (v. 21). David not only served the king in his court, soothing his troubled spirit with God's Word set to music (also a reflection of God's grace toward Saul), but he also became Saul's armor-bearer. This "man after God's own heart" was constantly in Saul's presence.

## God's Patience

God gave Saul many years to learn spiritual lessons—and to turn back to Him. This too displayed God's grace. Though the Lord had rejected Saul as king, He did not dethrone him immediately. He did not reject him as His child. David could have become Saul's deliverer and savior had the king humbled himself before God and truly repented. Those years of transition—from the time Saul was rejected until David became king —could have been Saul's happiest and most productive. Rather, they were his most miserable and disastrous, primarily because he continued to reject God's love and grace.

# *Questions Christians Ask*

## Will the Holy Spirit Ever Leave a Christian?

Saul's disobedience and the subsequent results raise several questions. When studying the ministry of the Holy Spirit in the Old Testament, it's imperative that Christians apply a New Testament perspective. After Jesus Christ returned to heaven, the Holy Spirit came upon certain individuals—particularly the apostles—in unusual ways, and anointed them with special power and gave them special messages. These experiences were similar to what God did for certain Old Testament leaders. However, when the Holy Spirit came on the Day of Pentecost, He came to *indwell* all people who sincerely put their faith in Jesus Christ as their Lord and Savior. Peter proclaimed for all to hear in Jerusalem that the promise of the Holy Spirit was for *everyone* who responded to the gospel message (Acts 2:39). Though the experiences associated with the presence of the Holy Spirit varied according to God's sovereign will, the promise was for all true Christians of all time. This is why Paul told the Corinthians, "For by one Spirit we were *all* baptized into one body" (1 Cor. 12:13). Paul also answered the above question very specifically when he wrote to the Ephesians: "In

Him, you also, after listening to the message of truth, the gospel of your salvation—having also believed, you were *sealed in Him* with the Holy Spirit of promise, who is given as a *pledge of our inheritance*, with a view to the redemption of God's own possession, to praise of His glory" (Eph. 1:13–14).

In Old Testament days, God gave His Spirit only to certain people whom He chose to serve as His prophets and special leaders. On rare occasions, however—as we've seen in Saul's case—the Holy Spirit departed from men.

Not so in the New Testament! Jesus said to His followers, "I will ask the Father, and he will give you another Counselor to be *with you forever*—the Spirit of truth" (John 14:16–17a, NIV).

When comparing the ministry of the Holy Spirit in Old Testament and New Testament days, we find at least three differences:

1. In Old Testament days, the indwelling presence of the Spirit related only to a special anointing on *those who were already His children.* In New Testament days, the indwelling presence of the Spirit related to *becoming God's children*—conversion to Jesus Christ.

2. In Old Testament days, the Spirit indwelt only *certain believers*; in New Testament days, the Holy Spirit indwells *all believers.*

3. In Old Testament days, under certain circumstances *God would remove* His Holy Spirit from an individual; in New Testament days, God has promised that His Spirit *would never leave* His children.

We can rest in the security of God's promises. He cannot lie!

## What about Demon Possession?

There are many cases of demon possession in the New Testament where Jesus encountered these people and healed them (Matt. 8:14–16). He also gave the apostles and other groups of Christians the same power to cast out demons (Matt. 10:1; Luke 10:17).

After Jesus' return to heaven, Paul also encountered these problems in his own ministry. In Philippi, he cast a demon out of the servant girl who followed him (Acts 16:16–18). In Ephesus, *many* people were delivered from evil spirits (19:8–12).

## Is There Such a Thing as Demon Possession Today?

I definitely believe demon possession exists today. I've encountered this phenomenon as a Christian counselor. However, I also believe that many problems attributed to demons actually are reflections of spiritual and psychological difficulties. Though the problems we face as human beings are a direct result of sin in the world, they are not in the most part caused by direct contact with Satan or evil spirits.

I've counseled a number of people over the years with very severe problems. In all of these cases, I've seen very few demon-possessed people. I must acknowledge, however, that my counseling has been limited to people (both Christians and non-Christians) who have been directly influenced by the message of Christianity. This is particularly true in our own culture. Whether modern historians, sociologists, and anthropologists admit it or not, Western culture in general and American culture in particular have been deeply affected by the teachings of the Old and New Testaments. Indeed, the Ten Commandments form the frame of reference for our laws.

Many missionaries who have ministered outside of the Western culture, however, have encountered people who are totally pagan in their religion and lifestyle. They are like those to whom Paul ministered in Ephesus. They're given over to idolatry. They actually worship evil spirits.

Many missionaries who have served in these cultures have observed demon possession. Though I believe some of the cases probably are also rooted in psychological disturbances, I am convinced that many are real and very similar to the kinds of problems Jesus and the apostles encountered when they walked the face of the earth.

There is no question that we have seen an increase in demonic activity in recent years in the United States. This is particularly related to the influence of the drug culture as well as certain aspects of New Age religion. Many people have opened their minds to the spirit world. Some actually worship Satan. When this happens, demon possession becomes a reality.

## Can a Christian Ever Become Demon-Possessed?

Some Christian scholars give a decided yes to this question; others give a decided no. And some believe that a Christian can be harassed, oppressed, or "demonized" by an evil spirit—but not possessed. The problem we face is that we have no definitive way to evaluate these experiences with biblical examples and direct teaching.

Personally, I tend to believe that a Christian *can* be controlled by demons. I can only verify this, however, from my personal experiences in counseling. This is particularly true when we encounter people who as children were subjected to Satanic ritual abuse. It also can happen when a Christian willfully turns his back on God and dabbles in the occult—as Saul perhaps did.

When all is said and done, perhaps our disagreements are merely semantic. One thing is certain, however: Satan is alive and well, and as Christians we must all put on the whole armor of God so we can take a stand against Satan's evil tactics. The Bible teaches that when we do, we can be victorious and win the battle against evil (Eph. 6:11–18).

James wrote: "Submit yourselves, then, to God. *Resist the devil, and he will flee from you.* Come near to God and he will come near to you" (James 4:7–8, NIV). This is a comforting promise.

## Becoming God's Man Today

*Principles to Live By*

Following are some lessons we can learn from Saul's awesome experience, especially when we compare what happened to him with teachings in the New Testament.

### *Principle 1. We must develop a correct view of God.*

God lovingly disciplines His children as a patient and kind heavenly Father. He is not out to punish us when we disobey Him. Remember that God has already forgiven us in Jesus Christ. His desire is that we now walk in His will. Once we become true believers, He will never take His Holy Spirit from us. His grace continues to reach out to us, long after we walk out of His will.

On the other hand, we must never take God's love and grace for granted. The Bible teaches that there comes a time when He gives people over to their own sinful desires. In this sense, every human being can determine his own destiny and will suffer the natural consequences of walking out of the will of God (Rom. 1:24–32). We reap what we sow—even as Christians (Gal. 6:7).

Paul also teaches that there will be Christians who are saved "only as one escaping through the flames" (1 Cor. 3:15, NIV). They will face the judgment seat of Christ without any rewards and gifts to offer back to their Savior. Personally, I don't want to stand before God under these circumstances. I want to love Jesus Christ as He loved me—as much as that is possible on this earth.

### *Principle 2. We must never dabble in the occult.*

Christians should never participate in activities that have any kind of supernatural dimensions other than those that relate to worshiping the one true God. This includes Ouija boards, astrological games and any other form of activity associated with the spirit world. Some of these activities—even certain forms of meditation—may appear harmless, but they also may be very dangerous, especially for people who are impressionable and/or psychologically distressed.

The Scriptures teach that we must "fix our eyes on Jesus, the author and perfecter of our faith" (Heb. 12:2, NIV). Let us resist Satan, knowing he will flee from us. Let us "stand firm then, with the belt of truth . . . with the breastplate of righteousness . . . and with [our] feet fitted with . . . the gospel of peace." Also let us "take up the shield of faith . . . [and] the helmet of salvation and the sword of the Spirit, which is the word of God." And finally we should "pray in the Spirit on all occasions" (Eph. 6:14–18, NIV).

### *Principle 3. We must guard against confusing psychological problems with demonic activity.*

As a general rule—particularly among people who have had no direct contact with the occult—persistent problems of anxiety, obsessions, compulsions, depression, and anger are rooted in personal problems that are psychological and spiritual in nature. To attribute these problems to Satan's direct influence can make them worse.

To attribute psychological problems to God's judgment also can be very devastating to an already emotionally disturbed person. We must remember that Saul's case was unique—no matter what the interpretation regarding the cause of his problem. It was definitely because of God's judgment. It does not represent the normal state of things when people have psychological difficulties.

#### *Obsessive Thoughts*

I have talked with people who have been plagued by obsessions—thoughts that continually intrude into their minds. Some of these people believe the obsessions come from Satan. Some believe they are from the Holy Spirit.

However, the more they resist the obsession, the more it dominates and controls them. This is a sure sign of a psychological obsession.

If these obsessions are from Satan, the Bible teaches us that if we resist them, he will leave us alone. Satan will flee from us. If the thoughts are from the Holy Spirit, when we pray He will certainly help us rather than cause the problem to get worse.

I counseled with a sincere Christian man who periodically became obsessed with thoughts that he did not love his wife. Knowing this young man well, I knew his obsession was false. He loved his wife dearly. However, he could not get these negative thoughts out of his mind when they intruded.

I advised this young man not to resist the thought but to accept it as a psychological obsession that was not based in fact. I also reassured him that I knew he loved his wife and gave him factual evidence for my conclusion. By taking this advice he was able to dissipate the obsession. However, if he fought the problem in his mind, it controlled him.

It's apparent from this illustration that the obsession had nothing to do with either the Holy Spirit or an evil spirit. It resulted from the influence of sin in the world and upon our lives. In essence, this obsession was rooted in his psychological nature.

### *The Problem of Guilt*

There are complex reasons why people experience obsessions. However, many times it goes back to guilt problems in childhood. A sensitive individual who has repressed these feelings often encounters obsessive thoughts later in life. In such cases, you cannot help a person overcome these problems by simply attributing the obsession to Satan or even to the Holy Spirit.

Another illustration helps explain why it is so vital to differentiate between problems rooted in the psychological and those that may be caused by a direct influence of Satan. One evening, following a church service, a young man approached me. He was in great emotional agony and asked that I—and others—pray for him. He told me with great conviction he believed that he was possessed by a demon.

There were several other pastors present in this service. I asked them to join me in prayer for this young man. One of the pastors immediately volunteered to take charge, indicating that he had previous experience casting out demons.

I was happy to fade into the background. I participated in the prayer service, but began to question what was happening. I noticed that after approximately an hour of what was supposed to be an exorcism, the young man was getting worse. He was experiencing increased frustration and his body contortions and distorted speech became even more noticeable.

While watching this process, I noted that some of his reactions had distinct psychological overtones. I asked if I might talk to the boy one-on-one. I knelt beside him and began to interpret his problem psychologically—particularly in terms of guilt and how it affects us. "Is God telling you what I'm thinking?" he asked, startled. "No," I said, "I'm simply interpreting your problem psychologically and emotionally."

Immediately the boy relaxed. His body contortions stopped. There was no more "growling" and slurred speech. After a few minutes, I asked the boy why he had gone through this physical display. His answer was more surprising than his quick recovery; he reported that since we believed he had a demon, he didn't want to disappoint us.

We were even more chagrined when he went on to tell us he had heard an evangelist speak about demon possession. The speaker had described very vividly how demons control people and how people react when they are possessed. This impressionable young man had identified his inner psychological struggles with what the evangelist had described as demon possession and was attempting to simulate it.

This man was not being flagrantly dishonest. He was sincerely trying to get at the root of his problem. He really believed he was demon-possessed. The fact is that he was psychologically disturbed—primarily because of extensive guilt over past and present sin in his life. The worship service he had been in with us confronted him with his guilt so severely that he actually felt he was being attacked by Satan. He began acting out what he had been taught by someone who graphically described demon possession.

Had we left this young man in a state of emotional and psychological turmoil, believing he had a demon that we could not cast out, it's frightening to think of what might have happened to him. This experience indelibly impressed on me how important it is to differentiate between problems that are psychological and spiritual in origin and those that are rooted in some type of demon possession. It's dangerous to dabble in demonism, including an attempt to exorcise or contact them.

Please don't misunderstand. This does not mean some people are not actually possessed. When they are, we must approach the problem differently. However, we must be wise in our response to these problems. Personally, I approach these situations first from a spiritual and psychological point of view. I try to eliminate those possibilities before concluding there is some type of supernatural, evil activity in a person's life.

### *An Actual Case of Demon Possession*

A counselor friend and I actually encountered a demon-possessed girl. She too had many bizarre emotional reactions. However, they did not fit the norm. She had been in psychiatric counseling for some time without success. The psychiatrist also acknowledged that this was not a normal situation that could be diagnosed with typical psychiatric definitions and approaches.

My friend and I consulted a man who was more experienced than we were in dealing with demonic activity. This person helped us to eliminate the psychological and emotional possibilities. We concluded that this individual was indeed demon-possessed, although she also had some deep psychological problems.

The major symptom that we faced was that this individual believed that Jesus Christ died for everyone except her. She was very consistent in this belief. Consequently, we began to pray a "warfare" prayer for her based on Ephesians 6. It was not a wild confrontation, with us shouting at Satan and the demons. Rather, we simply pleaded the blood of Christ and acknowledged that Jesus Christ had power over the evil forces that were troubling this girl. She initially resisted, but gradually relaxed and was able to listen to the Word of God. Her agitation ceased. As a result, for the very first time in her life she was able to acknowledge that Jesus Christ died for her. She accepted the Lord as her Savior and was born again. She was set free—free from her false beliefs and free to begin to work on the emotional difficulties she still faced in life.

## Becoming a Man after God's Heart

As you evaluate the following principles, pray and ask the Holy Spirit to impress on your heart one lesson you need to apply more effectively in your life. Then write out a specific goal. For example, you may have discovered that you do not have a correct view of God. You see Him more as a father who "punishes" than as a loving father who "disciplines."

___ We must develop a correct view of God.

___ We must never dabble in the occult.

___ We must guard against confusing psychological problems with demon activity.

*Set a Goal*

With God's help, I will begin immediately to carry out the following goal in my life:

___

___

___

___

## *Memorize the Following Scripture*

> *For I am convinced that neither death nor life, neither angels nor demons, neither the present nor the future, nor any powers, neither height nor depth, nor anything else in all creation, will be able to separate us from the love of God that is in Christ Jesus our Lord.*
>
> Romans 8:38–39, niv

Chapter 4

# *A Battle We Can Win!*

Read 1 Samuel 17:1–58

A number of years ago, a young man named Billy Graham was conducting evangelistic meetings in a large Ringling Brothers' circus tent in Los Angeles. Several prominent people made decisions for Christ, which caught the attention of newspaper magnate, William Randolph Hearst. Intrigued by what was happening, Hearst told his reporters to "puff Graham," to publicize this relatively unknown young evangelist.

Within days, the world knew about Billy Graham. He was soon featured in *Time*, *Newsweek,* and *Life*, giving him instantaneous international prominence.

The rest of the story is history. God used Mr. Hearst to open a door for worldwide outreach through the Billy Graham Evangelistic Association.

God sometimes uses the most unusual circumstances *and* people—even unbelievers—to achieve His purposes in this world. This is what happened to a young, relatively unknown shepherd boy named David. Even though he served as Saul's personal musician and carried the king's armor, few in Israel knew about his unusual skills and abilities. More importantly, they knew little about his relationship with God. But all that changed when he came face to face with a huge Philistine warrior named Goliath.

## *A Door of Opportunity*

The story of David and Goliath is one of the most dramatic events in the history of Israel. After the shepherd boy encountered the powerful Philistine warrior and won a decisive victory, he not only became a popular figure in Israel but also gained fame among the nations that surrounded God's chosen people. God provided David with a door of opportunity to prove himself —and David walked through the door!

### A Miraculous Victory

God had granted Israel a miraculous victory over the Philistine army. By all human standards, Israel should have been defeated. However, the Lord's blessing was still upon Saul and consequently upon Israel. Even though they were ill-equipped for war, God assisted Israel by sending an earthquake, creating terrible confusion in the Philistine camp (1 Sam. 14:12–23). Consequently, Israel won an unusual battle.

### The Philistines Regroup

Routed and defeated, the Philistines reorganized. They desperately wanted to defeat and capture Israel, and bring the nation under their dominion. They regrouped and once again "gathered their armies for battle." This time, however, they used a different tactic, one that was common in those days. Rather than taking a chance on losing a lot of lives as they did at Michmash, they confronted Israel with a single warrior—Goliath—challenging Saul to send a representative to fight him. The battle would be won or lost on the basis of two men battling each other. The losing side would voluntarily become servants of the victors.

The Philistine warrior stood at least nine feet, six inches tall. Even Saul, who was taller than any other man in Israel, was puny by comparison. Goliath's appearance and presence was an awesome sight! His shout alone created fear in the hearts of Saul's warriors (17:11).

## The Philistine Challenge

Every day, twice a day, for forty days, the huge Philistine descended to the valley floor and shouted up to the children of Israel, challenging someone to come and fight him. His words were clear and crisp—and very foreboding to Israel: "Why do you come out to draw up in battle array? Am I not the Philistine and you servants of Saul? Choose a man for yourselves and let him come down to me. If he is able to fight with me and kill me, then we will become your servants; but if I prevail against him and kill him, then you shall become our servants and serve us" (vv. 8–9).

The results were devastating. "When Saul and all Israel heard these words of the Philistine, they were dismayed and greatly afraid" (v. 11). There wasn't a man in the army of Israel who dared to accept the challenge. It would be suicide! Even their leader, Saul—the tallest of them all—was paralyzed with fear.

# *David's Moment*

Then the unexpected happened! David suddenly walked onto God's divine stage.

He had been fulfilling two jobs—playing his harp for Saul during the king's periods of depression and continuing his shepherd role. When Goliath first uttered his challenge, David was back home helping his father. However, some time during the forty days when Goliath appeared on the valley floor, Jesse asked David to take some food to his three older brothers serving in Saul's army—and to see how they were doing.

## "Who Is This Uncircumcised Philistine?"

David was startled when he arrived on the scene. He saw the huge Philistine descend from the mountain across the valley and heard him shout out his challenge to Israel. David's warrior heart stirred immediately. How could anyone have the gall to defy Israel and defame the name of God (v. 26)? To the amazement and chagrin of his fellow Israelites—particularly his brothers—David volunteered to accept the giant's bold invitation. He stood ready to defend the name of the Lord!

## "You Are but a Youth!"

Saul tried to convince David he wouldn't have a chance against Goliath. "You are not able to go against this Philistine to fight with him;" he said, "for *you are but a youth* while he has been a warrior from his youth" (v. 33). Saul believed David would be committing suicide; he couldn't possibly win.

## Saul's Limited Perspective

Saul didn't understand David. He didn't know about his special skills or comprehend his faith in God. Neither did he understand God's special blessing upon this young man. But when Saul saw that David was determined, he loaded him down with the king's own armor. But David knew he couldn't use his special skills with the extra weight. He needed freedom of movement. He stripped off the armor and descended into the valley to face the giant dressed only in his simple shepherd garb. He had nothing in his hands except a shepherd's staff, a sling and five smooth stones in a shepherd bag.

## Caught Off-Guard

Goliath was dumbfounded when he saw David coming out to meet him with no protection—not even a shield bearer. David had no armor or helmet to cover his youthful appearance and his flowing red hair. Goliath recognized immediately he was facing a boy—not a trained warrior.

Goliath's anger reached a fever pitch and in his humiliation, he cursed David. At this moment he may have thrown his helmet to the ground and faced David with an unprotected head. Whatever transpired, his guard was down. Quick as a flash—before the Philistine knew what was happening, a stone flew from David's sling and pierced the giant's forehead. Goliath crashed to the ground—dead!

## The Battle Was Over

The Philistine army watched in horror as David severed Goliath's head from his body with the great warrior's own sword. They all turned tail and fled, with the army of Israel in hot pursuit.

With this victory, David entered a new era in his life, particularly in his relationship to God's people. Though he had won a battle for Israel—and for the Lord—David's greatest battles in the future would be not against the enemies of Israel but against Saul. They would be with the man he honored and served. David was about to travel a very difficult road before he would become the recognized king of Israel.

# *What Goliath Teaches Us*

This mighty Philistine warrior had a view of himself and of life that teaches all of us—particularly men—many valuable spiritual lessons:

## Self-Confidence Alone Is a "Dead-End Street!"

Goliath's confidence focused on himself. He placed his faith in his huge frame, his strength—and his ability to wield his weapons.

The Bible records it well: "He had a bronze helmet on his head, and he was clothed with scale armor which weighed five thousand shekels of bronze. He also had bronze greaves on his legs and a bronze javelin slung between his shoulders. And the shaft of his spear was like a weaver's beam, and the head of his spear weighed six hundred shekels of iron; his shield-carrier also walked before him" (17:5–7).

## Arrogance Leads to Disaster!

Goliath appeared before Israel with total confidence in his ability to defeat and kill any man who dared to face him on the battlefield. "I defy the ranks of Israel," he shouted (v. 10).

This Philistine warrior was a self-centered man with an ego as huge as his frame. He believed no man could beat him. He was humiliated when "little David" approached him; it hurt his pride. His arrogance became his downfall! The apostle Paul put it well when he wrote to the Romans, "Through the grace given to me I say to every man among you not to think more highly of himself than he ought to think; but to think so as to have sound judgment" (Rom. 12:3).

## False "Gods" Will Fail Us

When David approached Goliath, the huge Philistine cried out in anger, "'Am I a dog, that you come to me with sticks?' And the Philistine cursed David *by his gods*" (1 Sam. 17:43).

Goliath, like all his compatriots, did not worship the one true God. The Philistines were deeply enmeshed in the Canaanites' religious culture and worshiped false gods such as Dagon and Baalzebub (Judg. 16:23–24; 1 Sam. 5:1–5; 2 Kings 1:2–6). Sadly, he believed idols made of stone could help him defeat the God who created the universe. He was spiritually blind.

## Tunnel Vision Sets Us Up for Deception

Because of Goliath's human and pagan philosophy of life, he was easily deceived. When David approached him with his shepherd garb and staff, and with a mere sling in his hand, he threw Goliath off-guard. The giant only understood warfare of a certain kind. Like lumbering modern armies facing quick guerrilla fighters, he wasn't prepared to defeat such a simple weapon as a slingshot. He only understood brute strength and how to use "a sword, a spear and a javelin" (1 Sam. 17:45). He had "tunnel vision."

## In Summary . . .

Goliath's perspective represents a man of this world. He knew nothing of trusting God and honoring Him with his life. His confidence rested purely in himself, his military skills, and his protective armor. He did not comprehend—or at least refused to acknowledge—the one true God. Consequently, Goliath was extremely vulnerable to a young man who didn't have the warrior's battle skills, but who knew how to use a sling. More importantly, David had a dynamic relationship with the living God.

## *What David Teaches Us*

David's perspective on life was diametrically opposed to Goliath's. He knew these truths:

### God's Reputation Must Always Be First

When Goliath taunted Israel, it bothered David tremendously—not so much because of his national pride, but because Israel represented God's chosen people. In David's mind, to attack Israel was to attack God.

More importantly, David wanted all people to know it was God who helped Israel win battles. He was determined that neither he nor anyone in Israel should ever take glory that belonged to the Lord. Thus he said: "This day *the LORD will deliver you up* into my hands . . . that all the earth may know that there is a God in Israel, and that all this assembly may know that the Lord does not deliver by sword or by spear; for *the battle is the LORD's* and He will give you into our hands" (vv. 46–47).

### Confidence in God Leads to Success

When Saul tried to convince David he could never defeat Goliath, David's response revealed his heart: "The LORD who delivered me from the paw of the lion and from the paw of the bear, *He will deliver me* from the hand of this Philistine" (v. 37). And as he approached Goliath, he called out, "You come to me with a sword, a spear, and a javelin, but I come to you in the name of the LORD of hosts, the God of the armies of Israel, whom you have taunted" (v. 45).

## Balance Is the Key

David knew he had unusual skills. He also knew his limitations. Saul's armor would interfere, not help. He knew he could throw a stone with accuracy. He had honed that skill for years while guarding his father's sheep. He believed his faith in God—combined with his ability to use the sling—would enable him to win the battle against Goliath. And he did!

This is one of the most difficult balances to maintain in life. I often find myself vacillating. When I feel good physically and mentally and my ability to produce is high, I tend to place confidence in my own strength. Then I have to experience difficulties and defeat to stop and ask God for His supernatural help.

As I've grown older, I've learned to maintain more balance in my Christian life. But I still struggle, depending on circumstances and situations. Most of us do! This is why we should remind ourselves daily to put on God's armor and be strong in His strength (Eph. 6:11–18).

## Opportunities Come when We're Prepared

David's skill with a sling wasn't an inherited ability. He spent many hours practicing out on the hillsides while performing his shepherding responsibilities. In those days a sling was really a secret weapon in Israel. Many learned to use it with accuracy. In the book of Judges we read of "700 choice men who were left-handed; each one could sling a stone at a hair and not miss" (Judg. 20:16).

The point: David *was prepared* for this moment of opportunity. When the time came, he walked through this open door, glorified his Lord—and saved his people from potential defeat!

# *Following the Way of Goliath*

If Saul represents a carnal Christian rebelling against God, Goliath clearly represents an unbeliever who doesn't know

God at all. Though the Philistine warrior certainly demonstrated this truth in the extreme, everything he did applies to the person who has not put his faith in Christ for salvation.

This certainly proved true in my own life as a non-Christian. I trusted in myself—my abilities, my talents, my capabilities. My security rested in my own accomplishments and in those material things I could accumulate in this world. This led me to pride and arrogance that stood in the way of recognizing God for who He is and what He wanted to do in my life.

True, I wasn't pagan in the sense that I explicitly denied God or Christ, but my false "gods" were myself, my friends, and material things. That's basically all I had to live for. I believed in God, but I had never bowed before Him, acknowledged my need for a Savior, and accepted His free gift of eternal life. Consequently, I was vulnerable to all kinds of failure. Because I trusted in myself, I was easily deceived and often disappointed.

## *What About You?*

Do you know Christ personally? Are you trusting in yourself and what you can do, or are you trusting in Jesus Christ to be your personal Savior? If not, why not accept Jesus Christ today?

### A Prayer of Acceptance

The following prayer will assist you in becoming a Christian. Pray it with meaning, using your own words if you like. I assure you on the authority of the Word of God that if you pray this prayer sincerely, Jesus Christ will become your Savior and your life will begin to change. Consider these important promises before you pray the following prayer:

- "All that the Father gives Me shall come to Me, and the one who comes to Me I will certainly not cast out" (John 6:37).
- "Draw near to God and He will draw near to you" (James 4:8).

Father, like Goliath of old, I, ________________ [your name], confess I have been trusting in myself to win the battles of life. I now humbly bow before you, acknowledge my sins of pride and self-righteousness, and put my faith in the Lord Jesus Christ to be my Savior from sin. Come into my heart and help me to change the direction of my life.

Signed ______________________________

Date ________________________________

## Becoming God's Man Today

*Principles to Live By*

### *Principle 1. One of our greatest concerns should be to uphold God's reputation.*

Many of us call ourselves "Christians," which means we claim to be followers of Jesus Christ. His name is our name! But how concerned are we that as His representatives on earth, we constantly and consistently bring honor to His name?

Note Paul's exhortation to the Corinthians: "So whether you eat or drink or whatever you do, do it all for the glory of God. Do not cause anyone to stumble, whether Jews, Greeks or the church of God—even as I try to please everybody in every way. For I am not seeking my own good but the good of many, so that they may be saved. Follow my example, as I follow the example of Christ" (1 Cor. 10:31–11:1, NIV).

### *Principle 2. We must first and foremost trust God to help us achieve our goals.*

In our achievement-oriented culture, it's easy to carry out tasks in our own strength, not realizing how important it is to trust God to help us. I find myself bypassing God when I feel I can do things myself, and calling upon Him only when I'm in over my head and can't possibly make it on my own.

God's desire is that we trust Him at all times. Note God's will in this matter as spelled out in the book of Proverbs:

"Trust in the LORD with all your heart, and do not lean on your own understanding. In all your ways acknowledge Him, and He will make your paths straight" (Prov. 3:5–6).

### *Principle 3. We must* balance *faith in God with confidence in ourselves and in our own abilities.*

The story of David facing Goliath beautifully balances this truth. On the one hand, he knew the battle was the Lord's. On the other hand, he had confidence he could defeat Goliath with his skill with a slingshot.

Some Christians go to two extremes. Either they sit around and wait for God to fight their battles, or they are out trying to win all by themselves. God wants us to balance faith and work in our lives—but always operating in the strength of the Lord!

### *Principle 4. We must be prepared to do what God wants to achieve through us at any given moment.*

I'm convinced that God bypasses some Christians because they fail to prepare for the times when God wants to use them in special ways. David illustrates preparedness. He developed his skill long before he needed it. And when the opportunity came, God used that skill in an extraordinary way.

How prepared are you for the time when God wants to do some very special things through your life—some things you cannot even imagine?

## Becoming a Man after God's Heart

As you evaluate the following principles, pray and ask the Holy Spirit to impress on your heart one lesson you need to apply more effectively in your life. Then write out a specific goal. For example, you may have difficulty in balancing faith in God with confidence in yourself and your own abilities.

____ One of our greatest concerns is to uphold God's reputation.

____ We must first and foremost trust God to help us achieve our goals.

____ We must balance faith in God with confidence in ourselves and our own abilities.

____ We must be prepared to do what God wants to achieve through us at any given moment.

*Set a Goal*

With God's help, I will begin immediately to carry out the following goal in my life:

______________________________________________

______________________________________________

______________________________________________

______________________________________________

*Memorize the Following Scripture*

*Now to Him who is able to do exceeding abundantly beyond all that we ask or think, according to the power that works within us, to Him be the glory in the church and in Christ Jesus to all generations for ever and ever. Amen.*

Ephesians 3:20–21

## Chapter 5

# *That Insidious "Giant" Called Jealousy*

Read 1 Samuel 17:57–58; 18:1–18

I'll never forget a challenge I faced as a young man playing high school basketball. My home school in a small Indiana town went up against a team from a much larger city. The man I guarded that night stood head and shoulders above me. I don't know what possessed me, but I decided to use my elbows illegitimately—which made this "giant" basketball player I was guarding furious. The next time down the court, he taught me a lesson I've never forgotten. He retaliated—and set the record straight. After reeling for a few minutes from a blow to the head, I thereafter humbly played by the rules.

This is about as close as I've ever come to physically taking on a "giant." Try as I might, I was never able to hold my own against this guy.

Few of us can identify with what David faced that day when he faced Goliath, since the huge Philistine may have been twice David's size. But all of us can identify with another "giant"—the powerful emotion we call "jealousy." We've either faced this temptation in our own lives or we've encountered it in others.

## *A Battle David Never Won*

David slew Goliath as King Saul's representative. Little did he realize that this heroic act would create a second "giant" that would become far more difficult to confront. Ironically, the second "giant" was Saul himself. Because of David's popularity, Saul became suspicious and jealous.

What made this problem particularly difficult for David was that Saul was supposedly a friend. Goliath was clearly an enemy.

Sadly, David never won this battle. Saul's jealousy lingered and grew worse until he died. But this is getting ahead of the story. What precipitated the jealousy? And what made it get worse?

## *Popularity Has Its Price*

Everyone in Israel admired David's great faith, courage, and skill. The people were instantly attracted to this young shepherd who dared to face the giant from Gath and save them from a humiliating defeat.

### Soul Brothers

Saul's own son, Jonathan, was probably more impressed with David's exploits than anyone else, creating a friendship that is unequaled in biblical history. A deep respect and rapport developed between these two young men. When Jonathan listened in on the conversation between his father and David following the victory over Goliath (1 Sam. 17:57–58), he recognized qualities of character he desired in himself. As the relationship grew, his soul "was knit to the soul of David, and Jonathan loved him as himself" (18:1).

### A Lifetime Covenant

Because of his admiration and love for David, Jonathan "made a covenant" with his newfound friend based on a mutual agreement. Jonathan and David vowed to be true and loyal friends the rest of their lives.

Jonathan sealed this contract with an act of kindness that is still considered in some parts of the world as the most significant honor one human being can bestow on another. As a prince, Jonathan clothed David with his own garments. He "stripped himself of the robe that was on him and gave it to David, with his armor, including his sword and his bow and his belt" (18:4).

## David's Promotion

Initially Saul also admired David and honored him with a promotion. David no longer served merely as the king's court musician and one of his armor-bearers. Rather, Saul "set him over the men of war" (v. 5).

Even Saul's servants revered David. This is a true test of popularity. Of all people, they could have become jealous, for David had been one of them. But they didn't—and this is a reflection of how maturely David must have handled himself following his victory and promotion.

## All Was Not Well

For awhile, it appeared that David had no enemies in Israel. But all was not well in Saul's heart. Though he had honored David outwardly, a struggle was brewing inwardly that would soon erupt. Jealousy that had been simmering in Saul's heart all along reached a boiling point. From the beginning, David's popularity had threatened Saul. He may have promoted David primarily to please Jonathan.

On the very day the army returned from battle against the Philistines, large numbers of women "came out of all the cities of Israel, singing and dancing." Joyful music filled the air as they played tambourines and other musical instruments (v. 6).

Though Saul was leading the procession, David received more honor than the king. Imagine Saul's emotions when he heard the women singing, "Saul has slain his thousands, and David his ten thousands" (v. 7). The words of this song triggered memories in Saul he wished he could forget—but couldn't.

Saul's initial feelings of jealousy soon turned to rage. Paranoia took over. The question he raised about David spoke volumes: "Now what more can he have but the kingdom?" (v. 8).

At this moment, Saul could not have helped but remember Samuel's pronouncement that the Lord had "sought out for Himself a man after His own heart" to replace him as king (13:14). He immediately saw prophetic fulfillment in David's popularity. The events unfolding before his eyes triggered those memories. But rather than turning to God and seeking His help to overcome his jealous rage, he took matters into his own hands and deliberately set out to hurt David.

## The Pain of Being Replaced

The severest form of jealousy normally emerges when the popularity of one person is superseded by the popularity of another. That's exactly what happened in Saul's case. He had been Israel's national hero. When he was anointed king, everyone shouted, "Long live the king!" (10:24). He had been a great warrior. The biblical record clarifies that fact: "Now when Saul had taken the kingdom over Israel, he fought against all of his enemies on every side, against Moab, the sons of Ammon, Edom, the kings of Zobah, and the Philistines; and wherever he turned, he inflicted punishment. And he acted valiantly and defeated the Amalekites, and delivered Israel from the hands of those who plundered them" (14:47–48).

David unintentionally challenged Saul's popularity when he slew Goliath. He was lauded for his great exploits in battle, and suddenly Saul's popularity was replaced by David's.

Saul's reactions are predictable. Under most circumstances, unless a person being replaced displays unusual maturity and humility, what happened between these two men can lead to the worst kind of jealousy. And this is what happened to Saul.

## Concurrent Emotions

At least three common emotions are associated with jealousy —and Saul experienced them all. First, he "became very *angry.*" He was very displeased with what the women were singing and responded, "They have ascribed to David ten thousands, but to me they have ascribed thousands. Now what more can he have but the kingdom?" (18:8).

The second emotion Saul faced was *suspicion.* He lost his objectivity. Paranoia dominated his mind. He was obsessed "from that day on" (v. 9).

Saul's third emotion was *fear,* which resulted when God protected David from Saul's wrath (v. 12).

## Irrational Reactions

Saul's jealousy was so intense that it led to irrational behavior. His rage became uncontrollable. He looked for an opportunity to kill David—to eliminate the very one who had ministered to him so wonderfully but who now threatened his position. Twice Saul literally thrust his spear at David while he was playing the harp—but on both occasions God protected David and he managed to sidestep Saul's weapon.

The king recognized that David was being guided and protected by a power greater than Saul's. He also knew the source of that power—for at one time he had experienced it himself. Consequently his anger turned to deep anxiety and fear. We read that he was "afraid of David, for the LORD was with him but had departed from Saul" (v. 12).

## Promotion or Demotion?

Rather than facing himself and acknowledging his intense jealousy toward David, Saul "removed him from his presence." He then "appointed him as his commander of a thousand" (v. 13).

On the surface, this appears to be another promotion. However, Saul, with his distorted mind, had developed an evil scheme. He was rational enough to know he would only make himself more unpopular in Israel if he personally killed David. He could destroy the object of his jealousy, but lose face with those he was trying to impress. He would only "shoot himself in the foot."

## Saul's Alternatives

Saul ruled out the idea of trying to kill David with his

own spear. God was protecting David—and he knew it. Sadly, this knowledge did not bring Saul to his knees.

Saul could have bowed his heart before God, acknowledged that David was to be his successor and do what he could to prepare the way for the Lord's choice. This, of course, would have been the alternative God wanted him to choose.

But Saul made a third choice—a plan to eliminate David without destroying his own reputation. What better way could he achieve this goal than to promote David, give him more responsibility on the battlefield and make himself look good for doing so? At the same time, Saul was hoping David would be killed by the Philistines. If it worked, Saul figured it would be a win-win strategy.

To make his plan work, Saul gave his older daughter to David to be his wife—with one major condition. David would have to "be a valiant man . . . and fight the LORD's battles." At the same time, Saul was thinking diabolical thoughts: "My hand shall not be against him, but let the hand of the Philistines be against him" (v. 17).

No matter what Saul did to eliminate David, however, God's protecting hand and blessing was continually upon this young man. We read that David prospered "in all his ways for the LORD was with him." And "when Saul saw that he was prospering greatly, he dreaded him"—that is, he feared him even more. Ironically, rather than decreasing David's popularity, Saul's actions only did the opposite. We read that "all Israel and Judah loved David, and he went out and came in before them" (vv. 14–16).

## *A Universal Problem*

Jealousy has always been a problem. In fact, it's an integral part of our biological and psychological development. It first appears as a part of our emotional and psychological makeup between the ages of one and two. Ironically, it appears almost at the same time as our capacity to show affection. In adults like Saul, it can lead to a love-hate relationship.

In this sense, jealousy is a normal emotion. But as we grow and develop, God wants us to learn to understand our feelings and handle them constructively and maturely. Part of that plan involves good modeling from our parents, followed by our Christian conversion and learning to experience God's power through His Word and His Holy Spirit.

### The Ideal vs. The Real

The reality, however, is that most of us as human beings often fall out of harmony with God's plan for emotional development. Even as Christians, we battle the old flesh patterns that attempt to dominate us and lead us into sin. Giving way to jealous feelings is a constant temptation.

### Are Feelings Sinful?

Feelings in themselves are neither good nor bad. It's what we do with these emotions that's important. If we allow negative feelings to persist and dominate us, they'll very quickly lead to sinful actions. This is what James had in mind when he wrote that "each one is tempted when, by his own evil desire, he is dragged away and enticed. Then, after desire is conceived, it gives birth to sin" (James 1:14–15 NIV).

## *How Saul Handled His Jealous Feelings*

God certainly understands jealous feelings. This was also true in Saul's case. Any man would have been threatened under the circumstances the king faced. But God also would have helped Saul deal with his feelings had he responded in the right way. Instead:

*He did not deal with the root problem.* Saul's main problem was pride and hardness of heart. He had never truly shown remorse for his earlier disobedience. Here Saul was given another opportunity, but he only hardened his heart more.

*He did not turn to God for help.* Saul did not turn to God with his feelings. As far as we know, he never asked God to change his heart attitude. Instead, he took matters into his own hands and actively fought against God's will.

*He did not seek help from others.* There is no evidence that Saul sought help from anyone. Why didn't he turn to his own son, Jonathan, who could have helped him? Pride kept him from doing what was right.

*He did not share his feelings of jealousy with David.* Saul could have told David exactly how he felt and sought his personal help. After all, if David could slay Goliath with God's help, he could have helped Saul. He was not Saul's enemy. He had no plan to upstage the king. But Saul made no effort to be honest with David.

Saul bypassed *all* the steps that are necessary when dealing with jealousy—or, for that matter, any negative emotion. He simply refused to face his problem. Consequently things went from bad to worse. They always do!

## *How David Handled Saul's Jealousy*

What could David have done to help Saul? More specifically, what *did* David do? Sadly, he didn't do much better than most of us do when facing jealousy in others. With all due respect to David—a man after God's heart facing a very difficult situation—he could have done one thing that he didn't do. He could have approached this "giant" with the same faith and confidence with which he faced Goliath.

*He did not seek God's wisdom.* It doesn't appear that David even asked God for wisdom in this situation. Somehow this kind of problem is more difficult to turn over to the Lord. To cry out that "the battle is the Lord's" when facing a literal Goliath is one thing; to make the same statement when facing a person with an emotional problem is another. This is particularly true when that emotional problem seems to be working for us rather than against us—as it was in David's situation. Saul's immature behavior only enhanced David's position in the eyes of the people. Putting it bluntly, Saul made David "look good"—and David knew it!

*Can you identify with David?* I can certainly think of times in my own life when I have fallen into the same trap as David. When we threaten someone with our own skills and abilities, there is always a certain degree of emotional satisfaction. This is another emotion that is neither right nor wrong. However, we can allow this emotion to lead us into sin. If we are not extremely careful, we'll use that situation for our own advantage.

I remember one particular experience. I knew I was outperforming my superior. And I *knew* that everybody else in the organization knew it, including the CEO. Consequently, I began to *enjoy* how much better I was doing than my superior. In fact, I was motivated to outdistance him even more!

Looking back on the situation, I now realize my immaturity and how wrong my motives were. Don't misunderstand; I shouldn't have allowed this threat and jealousy to deter me from doing my best. My feelings accompanying my success weren't even wrong. But I can now think of ways I could have helped my boss rather than working solely to enhance my own image. Ironically, had I taken the "high road," I would have made myself look better anyway.

I believe David—particularly as a young man—probably fell into this trap as well. The fact that he was "a man after God's own heart" did not exempt him from yielding to this kind of temptation.

## Becoming God's Man Today

*Principles to Live By*

The following principles translated into questions are designed to help all of us apply the lessons we can learn from David's life about handling personal jealousy:

## *Handling Personal Jealousy*

1. *Am I dealing with the root problem?* I need to ask myself whether or not I really want to solve the problem. We must be careful not to allow our hearts to deceive us at this point. If we're not careful, we can sometimes get caught up in our own ego needs—just as Saul did.

2. *Have I sincerely turned to God for help?* It takes wisdom to solve this kind of problem in our lives. We must remember what James said: "But if any of you lacks wisdom, let him ask of God, who gives to all men generously and without reproach, and it will be given to him" (James 1:5).

3. *Have I sought help from other mature Christians?* All of us need help from other members of the body of Christ. Every Christian man needs an accountability partner—another man with whom he can safely share his deepest struggles. We need another man's prayers, wisdom and questions about how we're doing. This is accountability!

4. *Have I shared my feelings with the other person involved, confessing my sin and asking for his forgiveness and prayers?* We must understand that other people understand jealous feelings—even those who cause jealousy in us. Obviously, there are some people who would take advantage of our feelings and our honesty and vulnerability. However, they are few and far between. Most people will help us overcome these feelings—even when they happen to be the one of whom we're jealous.

## *Handling Jealousy in Others*

1. *What are my motives? Am I using this person's weakness to enhance my own image?* It doesn't take too much introspection to come to grips with the answer to these questions. Most of us know when we are building ourselves up by tearing someone else down. Though we should never allow another person's weaknesses to keep us from performing at a high level, there is

a way to approach the situation with motives that are noble rather than destructive.

2. *Have I sought advice from another mature Christian?* The key word here is "mature." During the personal experience I shared earlier, a Christian man who had a relatively high position in another organization advised me to "outdistance" my superior—to make him *really* look bad. It was not good advice. And I know now that he was not a *mature* Christian. In fact, his advice got other young men into serious trouble as well!

3. *Do I pray for this person regularly?* This is a real "motive tester." When we know someone is jealous of us—and that our performance is causing that jealousy—it becomes difficult to pray sincerely that the other person will be successful. And yet this is what God wants. Jesus actually taught us to pray for our enemies (Matt. 5:44).

*4. If the person is a Christian, have I faced the problem as God says I should?* Consider the following words of Jesus:

> "And why do you look at the speck in your brother's eye, but do not notice the log that is in your own eye? Or how can you say to your brother, 'Let me take the speck out of your eye,' and behold, the log is in your own eye? You hypocrite, first take the log out of your own eye, and then you will see clearly enough to take the speck out of your brother's eye." (Matt. 7:3–5)
>
> "And if your brother sins, go and reprove him in private; if he listens to you, you have won your brother. But if he does not listen to you, take one or two more with you, so that by the mouth of two or three witnesses every fact may be confirmed. And if he refuses to listen to them, tell it to the church; and if he refuses to listen even to the church, let him be to you as a Gentile and a tax-gatherer." (Matt. 18:15–17)

Consider also the words of Paul:

> Brethren, even if a man is caught in any trespass, you who are

spiritual, restore such a one in a spirit of gentleness; each one looking to yourself, lest you too be tempted. Bear one another's burdens, and thus fulfill the law of Christ. (Gal. 6:1–2)

## Becoming a Man after God's Heart

As you evaluate the following principles for handling jealousy in yourself or in others, ask the Holy Spirit to impress on your heart one lesson you need to apply more effectively in your life. Then write out a specific goal. For example, you may not be dealing with the root problem, and now realize that in your heart you really don't want to solve it.

*Principles for Handling Personal Jealousy*

____ I must deal with the root problem.
____ I must sincerely turn to God for help.
____ I must seek help from other mature Christians.
____ I must share my feelings with the other person involved, confessing my sin and asking for forgiveness and prayers.

*Principles for Handling Jealousy in Others*

____ I must not use this person's weakness to enhance my own image.
____ I must seek advice from another mature Christian.
____ I must pray for this person regularly.
____ I must remove the "log" from my own eye before I try to take the "speck" out of my brother's eye.

*Set a Goal*

With God's help, I will begin immediately to carry out the following goal in my life:

________________________________________

________________________________________

________________________________________

________________________________________

## *Memorize the Following Scripture*

> ***No temptation has overtaken you but such as is common to man; and God is faithful, who will not allow you to be tempted beyond what you are able, but with the temptation will provide the way of escape also, that you may be able to endure it.***
>
> 1 Corinthians 10:13

Chapter 6

# *David's Soul Brother*

Read 1 Samuel 13:15–23; 14:1–23; 18:1–4; 19:1–17; 20:1–42

What is true friendship? How does it develop? And how is it expressed? These questions, whether we verbalize them or not, are asked in the heart of most human beings. God created us to be social creatures; without friends our cup of life is only half-full. Most of us have lots of acquaintances—but how many of us have true friends?

## *True Friends*

The relationship that developed between David and Jonathan answers these questions better than any other source I know. The best definition of true friendship I've ever read is in the following description: "The soul of Jonathan was knit to the soul of David, and Jonathan loved him as himself" (1 Sam. 18:1).

The word *knit* literally means "chained." Think about that—the soul of Jonathan was "chained" to the soul of David. They were bound to each other in an inseparable relationship and union. In their minds and hearts they became one. They were "soul brothers." Though the friendship was initiated by Jonathan, David quickly responded with deep love and commitment. A friendship that flows only one way is really no friendship at all.

Rest assured that this was not a homosexual union as some liberal Bible interpreters suggest. If it were, what happened between David and Jonathan would clash with the law of God which commands, "You shall not lie with a male as one lies with a female; it is an abomination (Lev. 18:22).

The apostle Paul extended this prohibition into the New Testament era, identifying homosexual relationships as "indecent acts" that result in serious consequences (Rom. 1:26–27). To believe and teach otherwise is to deny the clear teachings of Scripture. David and Jonathan had a pure relationship that bound them together in a true friendship focused on God and their deep love for Him.

## *It Didn't Just Happen*

How did this God-honoring friendship develop? After all, there was a great social chasm between these two young men. David was just a shepherd boy and Jonathan a prince. From an economic, political, and social point of view, they had little in common.

### A Common Factor

Though in many respects there was a "great gulf fixed" between these two men, they had a common bond. They were both men after God's heart. They both had a dynamic relationship with their Lord. When their souls were knit together as one, their union was not merely another human relationship; it was a friendship based on a mutual love for God.

### Jonathan Was Impressed with David's Faith

Jonathan was greatly impressed with David from the very moment the young shepherd boy accepted the challenge to fight Goliath. Perhaps he had considered accepting this challenge himself, and on the same basis as David. He too knew that the battle would have to be the Lord's. Perhaps David simply beat him to the draw, for Jonathan's view of God's power was the same as David's. He had experienced it himself in a previous battle with the Philistines. The parallels between Jonathan's experience and David's are very clear.

## Jonathan's Previous Experience

Israel faced a formidable enemy. The Philistines were equipped with shields, cloaks of armor, spears, and javelins. Economically, they specialized in developing instruments made of iron and other metals. To add to Israel's predicament, the Philistines had captured out of Israel every blacksmith they could find, so the Israelites couldn't possibly equip themselves for battle with normal instruments of warfare (1 Sam. 13:19). The problem became so acute that every man in Israel had to rely on the Philistines to "sharpen his plowshare, his mattock, his axe, and his hoe" (v. 20).

Israel was economically dependent on the Philistines. They couldn't even plow their fields and harvest their crops without assistance from their enemies. At this point, they were only one step from becoming servants to the Philistines.

## Moving in for the Kill!

Israel's back was against the wall! In the midst of this economic crisis—and with Israel's army unprepared for war—the Philistines planned to attack them and to finish the job once and for all. Humanly speaking, Israel was doomed to disaster; it was just a matter of time. The Philistines were moving in for the kill from three directions (vv. 17–18).

## Jonathan's Step of Faith

Before Jonathan ever knew about David's personal relationship with God, he also believed "the battle is the Lord's." He too had a vital relationship with God.

Jonathan was one among a few who had any armor and weapons of warfare whatsoever. Without consulting anyone—not even his father—he decided one time to take on the whole Philistine army single-handedly (14:1). His only human assistant was his personal armor-bearer. This, of course, was a far greater challenge than David taking on Goliath.

## "The Lord Is Not Restrained"

Jonathan, like David, believed with all his heart that God could win the battle for him. Reassuring the young man carrying his armor, he beckoned, "Come and let us cross over to the garrison of these uncircumcised; perhaps the Lord will work for us, for *the LORD is not restrained to save by many or by few*" (v. 6). Jonathan knew it would be a simple matter for God to deliver the whole Philistine army into his hands.

## Waiting on God

But Jonathan didn't proceed on blind faith. He knew he couldn't conceivably win this battle without God's supernatural power. So he asked the Lord for a clear signal—a sign that God would indeed win this battle for him.

The Scriptures do not give us the exact details on how Jonathan discovered God's specific plan for approaching the Philistines. However, it's clear that he knew what to look for. He told his armor-bearer that they should move forward and reveal themselves to their enemies. If the Philistines told them to wait until they approached the pair, they would know they shouldn't proceed. However, if the Philistines asked the two to come on up to meet them, they would know the Lord approved of what they were doing. "This shall be the sign to us," said Jonathan (v. 10).

## The Plan Unfolds

When Jonathan and his armor-bearer made themselves visible to their enemies, they were invited to come out and meet them. This is the sign they were looking for. Jonathan moved forward with great confidence and faith—but also with humility. "Come up after me," he called to his armor-bearer, "for the LORD has given them into the hands of Israel" (v. 12).

## Reflections of Jericho

Years before, when Joshua led the children of Israel to attack Jericho, he also experienced a supernatural victory. He simply marched around the city seven days and on the seventh day, the walls came crashing down.

Jonathan was about to see a similar miracle. To start with, he and his armor-bearer killed twenty men. God then won the battle supernaturally by allowing a gigantic "trembling in the camp, in the field, and among all the people. Even the garrison and the raiders trembled, and the earth quaked so that it became a great trembling" (v. 15).

The Philistines were so baffled, confused, and shaken—literally and emotionally—that they fled in all directions. The Israelites followed in hot pursuit. That day the "LORD delivered Israel" (v. 23). It was a miraculous victory. God had honored Jonathan's faith. In his heart, Jonathan knew that the battle had been the Lord's!

## Like-Minded Hebrew Brothers

Later, as Jonathan stood in the wings watching David accept Goliath's challenge, and then saw him single-handedly slay the giant, his heart and mind flooded with memories of his own experiences when God had delivered the Philistines into Israel's hands. He immediately identified with David's experience and felt his soul strangely drawn to this God-honoring Hebrew brother. They had something in common, something very important. They both were men with hearts in tune with God. They knew the Lord personally and understood His greatness.

Perhaps more important than anything, they had a clear understanding of God's commitment to Israel. Both knew beyond a shadow of doubt that they were fighting the Lord's battle—not their own. There was no way they could have succeeded in their own strength.

The friendship that developed between Jonathan and David was no ordinary friendship. It's true that all the human elements were there—emotion, respect, admiration, commitment—but interweaving these human factors was a divine dimension that made this Old Testament friendship one of the most significant relationships in human history.

## *Marks of True Friendship*

What are the marks of true friendship? They're all here in this marvelous story. As we'll see, the focus is primarily on Jonathan. Because he was a prince, he had to take the initiative.

### He Honored David above Himself

Jonathan not only initiated this friendship, but also took the lead in establishing it on a solid foundation. Since he was a prince and David a subject, there was no other alternative. To the surprise of all who looked on, Jonathan "stripped himself of the robe that was on him [his royal robe] and gave it to David, with his armor, including his sword and his bow and his belt" (18:4).

To honor another person above yourself when you are social equals is one thing. To do so in Jonathan's situation is yet another. Here was a son of a king honoring a son of a shepherd!

Jonathan apparently recognized in David a man who had even greater personal courage and confidence in God than he had. Perhaps David had done what Jonathan had hesitated to do—and done it without armor, shield, or sword.

Jonathan was well aware of the implications of what he was doing. He was heir to the throne of Israel, but with this act of humility, he was willing to step aside to make way for his *friend.* He truly believed David could do the job better than he could. This attitude in Jonathan is verified later when he said to David, "You will be king over Israel and I will be next to you" (23:17). Jonathan was doing what his father should have done!

## A Faithful Intercessor

As the days went by, Saul's jealousy continued to flare. He tried various "backdoor" ways to kill David but each time he failed. He finally came to the point where he didn't care who knew his intentions. He made it an open issue. He even told Jonathan and all his servants what he wanted to do. In fact, he ordered *them* to do this evil deed (19:1).

Jonathan did not stand idly by. He went to work immediately to thwart his father's plan. First he warned David (v. 2). Then he went directly to his father and began to intercede for his beloved friend. "Do not let the king sin against his servant David," he pleaded. "He has not sinned against you, . . . his deeds have been very beneficial to you. For he took his life in his hand and struck the Philistine, and the LORD brought about a great deliverance for all Israel; you saw it and rejoiced. Why then will you sin against innocent blood, by putting David to death without a cause?" (vv. 4–5).

Jonathan touched a soft spot in his father's heart. Saul changed his mind—temporarily—and promised Jonathan he wouldn't follow through on his plans to kill David. Jonathan, true friend that he was, personally escorted David back into Saul's presence to serve the king both as his private musician and as an army officer (v. 7).

## A Friend—No Matter What

Unfortunately, Jonathan's success in building a bridge between his father and David was only an interim solution. During a horrible fit of rage while David was playing his harp, Saul once again tried to pin David to the wall with his spear. But David was too quick for the king's unsteady arm and once again sidestepped Saul's spear and "slipped away" (v. 10).

Saul's rage only exploded even more. He was not to be denied this time. He pursued David and sent a delegation to his house with an order to kill him. But, with the help of his wife, Michal, David once again escaped (vv. 11–17).

## David's Intense Fear

After fleeing from Saul, David visited the prophet Samuel in Ramah. Then he went to consult with Jonathan. At this point we begin to see the wear and tear on David's emotions. He had become very disturbed and threatened. This is understandable. He feared for his life. He felt he couldn't even continue to trust Jonathan's interpretation of Saul's motives. He trusted in Jonathan's integrity, but he believed Saul was no longer telling Jonathan the truth (20:3).

## A True Test

In the midst of this incredible tension, Jonathan proved faithful again. He was willing to do *anything* David asked (v. 4). Together they devised a scheme to test Saul's motives. They agreed that David would be absent from his regularly scheduled meal with the king. If Saul reacted with anger, they would know he had not changed his mind or heart.

David's instincts were right. When Saul noticed David was absent, he became so angry that he tried to kill his own son Jonathan—accusing him of protecting David. His words were cruel and harsh: "You son of a perverse, rebellious woman! Do I not know that you are choosing the son of Jesse to your own shame and to the shame of your mother's nakedness? For as long as the son of Jesse lives on the earth, neither you nor your kingdom will be established. Therefore now, send and bring him to me, for he must surely die" (vv. 30–31).

## The Die Was Cast

With this horrible outburst, Saul informed Jonathan in no uncertain terms that if he didn't help him find and kill David, he'd lose his right to the throne. Jonathan, however, had already settled that issue. He knew David was to be the next king of Israel—that he was "God's anointed."

Even in the midst of Saul's harsh attack, Jonathan stood his ground against his father's outburst. He interceded for David, which only infuriated Saul all the more. We read that the king "hurled his spear" at his own son in order "to strike him down."

That was the final blow. Jonathan knew "that his father had decided to put David to death" (v. 33). His angry outbursts had turned into a determined plot. Jonathan could no longer trust his father. He had to tell David the truth: from that point forward David would be a fugitive.

## A Sad Scene

David's heart was broken when Jonathan told him what had happened. They both knew it meant separation. Jonathan had no choice but to be loyal to his father, and David would certainly have had it no other way. But the decision was a difficult one for both of them. They wept and kissed each other as they parted, and though they would see very little of each other from that moment onward, they were never separated in their hearts. They were true friends—and true friends are friends forever.

## Becoming God's Man Today

*Principles to Live By*

The relationship between David and Jonathan constitutes an Old Testament picture of a New Testament reality—the relationships God intended to exist in the Body of Jesus Christ. What characterized this unique friendship in Israel was to be a norm in the church.

### *Principle 1. We are to be one in heart and soul.*

The Scriptures clearly teach that David and Jonathan were of "one soul." Compare this experience with the following New Testament references to relationships that should exist in the Body of Christ:

- "All the believers were one in heart and mind" (Acts 4:32, NIV).

- "May the God who gives endurance and encouragement give you a spirit of unity among yourselves as you follow Christ Jesus, so that with *one heart and mouth* you may glorify the God and Father of our Lord Jesus Christ" (Rom. 15:5, NIV).
- "Be of *one* mind" (2 Cor. 13:11, NIV).
- "Stand firm in *one* spirit, contending as *one* man" (Phil. 1:27, NIV).
- "Make my joy complete by being *like-minded*, having the same love, being *one* in spirit and purpose" (Phil. 2:2, NIV).

*Principle 2. We are to love others as we love ourselves.* David and Jonathan loved each other as they loved themselves. Again, compare this Old Testament relationship with New Testament injunctions:

- "Be devoted to one another in brotherly love" (Rom. 12:10).
- "Love your neighbor as yourself" (Rom. 13:9; Gal. 5:14).
- "Follow the way of love" (1 Cor. 14:1, NIV).
- "Keep on loving each other as brothers" (Heb. 13:1, NIV).
- "Love one another deeply, from the heart" (1 Pet. 1:22, NIV).

The relationship between David and Jonathan was clearly prophetic. In Jesus Christ, Christian brothers (and sisters) have the potential for true and enduring friendships that can never be equaled on this earth. True, all human beings can experience "friendships" because we are made in God's image. But only Christians have the potential for the quality of relationship that existed between David and Jonathan. The reason is that this relationship was focused both in God and man. In Christ, it's possible to experience a deep commitment to each other.

*Principle 3. We are to honor one another, be devoted to one another and even be willing to lay down our lives for one another.*

David and Jonathan's friendship parallels New Testament injunctions to members of Christ's Body:

| DAVID AND JONATHAN'S RELATIONSHIP: | RELATIONSHIPS WITHIN CHRIST'S BODY: |
|---|---|
| 1. Jonathan honored David above himself. | 1. Paul wrote to the Romans: "Honor One another above yourselves" (Rom.12:10, NIV). |
| 2. Jonathan served as a faithful intercessor. He was devoted to David. He served him and did everything he could to help David build a relationship with his father. | 2. Paul wrote: "Be devoted to one another" (Rom. 12:10). "Serve one another in love" (Gal. 5:13, NIV). "If one member suffers, all the members suffer with it" (1 Cor. 12:26). |
| 3. Jonathan continued to be faithful to David no matter what the cost to him personally. His life was in jeopardy when he tried to defend David's absence. | 3. John wrote in his First Epistle, "This is how we know what love is: Jesus Christ laid down his life for us. And we ought to lay down our lives for our brothers" (1 John 3:16, NIV). |

*Accountability Partners*

All of us in the Body of Christ are to develop friendships with each other, but it's also important to have one or two people in our lives who are even closer friends. Among men, this can take the form of an accountability partner. I recently returned from a men's retreat sponsored by my own church—Fellowship Bible Church North in Plano, Texas. Two men shared publicly that they had been accountability partners for a long time. However, one of them was moving from Dallas to

Houston. With tears, they told what the separation would mean —sadness. However, they both knew the move was best for this man's family.

That day we all saw a demonstration of true friendship between two brothers in Christ. They had shared their deepest joys and most difficult struggles. Consequently both men were better husbands, better fathers and better churchmen because of this friendship.

## Becoming a Man after God's Heart

As you evaluate your relationships with other members in the Body of Christ, pray and ask the Holy Spirit to impress on your heart one lesson you need to apply more specifically in your life. Then write out a specific goal. For example, perhaps you're constantly tempted to honor yourself above others. You now realize this is a violation of God's will for your life.

1. What kind of friend am I to other Christians generally?
   ____ Do I do all I can to be one in heart and mind with other believers?
   ____ Do I honor others above myself?
   ____ Am I loyal to my friends no matter what the cost to me personally?
   ____ How willing would I be to lay my own life on the line for a Christian brother or sister?
2. What kind of friend am I to those who are closest to me —my parents, my spouse, my children, my brothers and sisters?

*Set a Goal*

With God's help, I will begin immediately to carry out the following goal in my life:

______________________________________________

______________________________________________

______________________________________________

______________________________________________

*Memorize the Following Scripture*

> *We know love by this, that He laid down His life for us; and we ought to lay down our lives for the brethren.*
>
> 1 JOHN 3:16

Chapter 7

# *The Bible Tells It Like It Is*

Read 1 Samuel 19:18–24; 20:1–42; 21:1–15; Psalm 34

"I find it tremendously comforting," wrote the late Dr. Alan Redpath, "that the Bible never flatters its heroes. It tells the truth about them no matter how unpleasant it may be, so that in considering what is taking place in the shaping of their character we have available all the facts clearly that we may study them."[1]

## *David's Slide from Faith to Fear*

In our study of David's life, we have noticed his strengths. He was called a man after God's heart—one of the greatest tributes a person could ever receive. The Spirit of the Lord was upon him mightily. Against impossible odds, he faced Goliath and slew him, which was only the beginning of his great exploits in doing battle against the Philistines. He was known in Israel as a man of unusual courage and great faith in God.

But all was not well in David's heart and life. A change was gradually taking place. Little by little his faith in God's protection was being replaced by fear of what one man could do to him. And that man was King Saul!

David's fear *is* understandable—even predictable. He had faithfully served Saul as one of his armor-bearers and as his personal musician. At one time the king had demonstrated great love toward him (1 Sam. 16:21). But when David was honored by the people of Israel for his great victory over Goliath, Saul's love turned to intense jealousy, anger, and suspicion. He actually looked for opportunities to kill David.

Foiled in his murder attempts, Saul planned David's death on the battlefield by giving him greater military responsibility. Again, Saul's scheme failed. Repeatedly, he tried to "pin David to the wall" with his spear. But each time, David escaped. Saul's anger became relentless. He sent his own men to kill David. But David, with his wife's help, escaped through a window and fled.

Saul's attempts on David's life were becoming more frequent and intense. It was no longer a private scheme but a public strategy. And no one—including God Himself—would blame David for fleeing from Saul's presence. It was the only sensible thing to do.

There is no doubt David was under tremendous pressure. Few men would have—or could have—handled the situation the way he did. God certainly understood these difficulties.

However, there is another perspective. How David responded inwardly to these pressures and—more significantly—how he responded to God's protection is another matter. Rather than trusting the Lord as he had done so frequently in difficult situations, he began to lose his spiritual and emotional bearings. His most serious mistake: he ignored God's protection and he took matters into his own hands. When he did, things went from bad to worse.

## A Spiritual Mentor Fails

When David slipped out of his house through a window and escaped from Saul's men, he fled to Ramah (19:18). There he met and talked with the prophet Samuel. David apparently poured out his fears and frustrations to this old man who had anointed him to be the second king of Israel. But, it doesn't appear that Samuel was much help. Perhaps the prophet was so filled with fear of Saul himself that he couldn't encourage David or help restore his faith.[2]

It's not clear exactly what transpired between David and Samuel, but it's obvious from the text that God was willing and able to protect David from Saul—just as he had delivered him from his enemies on many previous occasions.

## A Strange Intervention

When Saul heard that David was at Ramah, he immediately sent men to capture him. When they arrived, they saw Samuel and a company of prophets prophesying before God. And lo and behold, the Spirit of the Lord came upon Saul's men and they also began to prophesy. Though we cannot be sure of all the dynamics, evidently these men were supernaturally thwarted by God in carrying out Saul's orders (v. 20).

Saul heard what had happened, and sent more men. The same thing transpired. In his unabated hostility and determination, Saul sent a third company of men—only to hear that the Spirit of God came upon them as well and stopped them from taking David captive (v. 21).

Saul's next move was to go to Ramah himself and capture David personally. But when he arrived, the Spirit of God came upon him also and so overpowered him that he lost control of his own will and prophesied along with the other prophets (vv. 23–24).

These are strange events, but they are in harmony with God's love in reaching out to men, no matter what their sins. In fact God was communicating two very important messages.

## God Was Still Reaching Out to Saul

When the Spirit of God came upon Saul and his men, the Lord was certainly reminding Saul of a very special event earlier in his life. Soon after he was anointed king, "the Spirit of God came upon him mightily, so that he prophesied among" the prophets (10:10). The question the people asked at that time was the same question they asked in Ramah: "Is Saul also among the prophets?" (10:11; 19:24).

How could Saul miss the message of this divine intervention? He was not just fighting David—he was fighting God! God was saying, loud and clear, that he was still able to change Saul's heart and life permanently—if only Saul would let Him.

### God Would Deliver David

The second message was for David: God could and would protect and deliver him from Saul. The Lord visually and dramatically demonstrated this fact. Without God's permission, Saul and his men could not touch David. God was showing David that He would protect him just as He had when David confronted Goliath. Sadly, David missed this message—just as Saul missed the message to him.

## *A Heart That Pulsated with Anxiety*

David's response to God's intervention on his behalf was anything but positive. As we've already noted, when he returned to talk to his friend Jonathan, he was emotionally and spiritually disturbed. His questions reflected confusion, doubt, and tremendous anxiety:

- "What have I done?
- "What is my iniquity?
- "And what is my sin before your father, that he is seeking my life?" (20:1).

When Jonathan tried to answer these questions positively and reassure him, David remained skeptical and nervous.

In fairness to David, we must acknowledge that he was right about Saul. Jonathan *was* deceived. David may have been frightened and anxious, but he had an accurate picture of his relationship with the king of Israel. Saul hated him desperately and was determined to take his life.

David's problem was that he didn't trust God to protect and deliver him. He had lost perspective on the past. What about "the lion," "the bear" and "the giant Goliath"? Seemingly, he even ignored what had just transpired in Ramah, when God intervened and protected him from Saul. Lost in a maze of his current circumstances, he proceeded to take matters into his own hands. The results were tragic!

## David's First Scheme

David first attempted to solve his problem by issuing this order to Jonathan: "Behold, tomorrow is the new moon, and I ought to sit down to eat with the king. But let me go, that I may hide myself in the field until the third evening. If your father misses me at all, then say, 'David earnestly asked leave of me to run to Bethlehem his city, because it is the yearly sacrifice there for the whole family.' If he says, 'It is good,' your servant shall be safe; but if he is very angry, know that he has decided on evil" (20:5–7).

*Where was God in this plan?* In devising this scheme, *David didn't consult the Lord at all.* In fact, the Lord's name isn't even mentioned in the plan.

How opposite from David's attitude and actions when he faced Goliath! At that time he said to Saul with great confidence, "The LORD who delivered me from the paw of the lion and from the paw of the bear, He will deliver me from the hand of this Philistine" (17:37). And when he encountered the giant face to face, David shouted, "I come to you *in the name of the LORD of hosts,* the *God* of the armies of Israel. . . . This day the *LORD* will deliver you up into my hands . . . that all the earth may know that there is a *God* in Israel, and that all this assembly may know that the *LORD* does not deliver by sword or by spear; for the battle is the *LORD's* and *He* will give you into our hands" (vv. 45–47).

*What happened to David's God-consciousness?* Somehow, some way, David had lost his spiritual bearings. The David we once knew would have said to Jonathan that day—"This struggle between your father and me is the *LORD's.* He will deliver me just as He did in Ramah." Instead, he came up with his own scheme. He left God out of the picture.

*There also was an element of dishonesty in David's strategy.* True, he may have planned to go to Bethlehem to sacrifice with his family someday, but there's no evidence he ever did or that he really planned to go at that moment. Furthermore, David asked Jonathan to give the impression he had already gone to Bethlehem (20:27–29), when in reality he was waiting "in the field" for a report on Saul's behavior (v. 24).

This was just the beginning of David's verbal distortions. One lie often leads to another—and this is exactly what happened to David.

## David's Second Scheme

Though David's scheme was purely a human strategy, it achieved its purpose. Saul's anger raged so out of control when he discovered David wasn't coming to his special luncheon that he attempted to kill Jonathan instead (v. 33). But his son escaped and went into the field to deliver the bad news to his beloved friend. In David's mind, he had no choice. Once again he fled—this time to the Tabernacle in Nob.

*Another Fabrication.* Ahimelech, the priest, was surprised to see David—especially since he was traveling all alone (21:1). In his panic, David once again took matters into his own hands. He took advantage of Ahimelech's surprise and quickly fabricated another story: "The king has commissioned me with a matter, and has said to me, 'Let no one know anything about the matter on which I am sending you and with which I have commissioned you'" (v. 2). In other words, he gave Ahimelech the false impression that he was alone because he was on a secret mission for King Saul.

*"Be sure your sins will find you out."* This time things didn't work out as nicely as David had hoped. Though he fooled Ahimelech, one of Saul's chief shepherds, Doeg the Edomite,

also was in Nob that same day and saw David. Word soon got back to Saul.

The results of David's sin in this case were tragic. Saul immediately called for Ahimelech and his whole family of priests. The king was irate and irrational. He accused Ahimelech of protecting David and helping him escape. No explanation would suffice. He ordered Ahimelech's death as well as the death of all the priests present that day—eighty-five men (22:18). The king also ordered an attack on the city of Nob and his men struck "both men and women, children and infants; also oxen, donkeys, and sheep" (v. 19). They wiped out the entire city.

*What a Price to Pay!* All this happened because David took matters into his own hands and lied. Later he acknowledged to a lone survivor, Abiathar, that he had "brought about the death of every person" in Nob (vv. 22–23). He took responsibility, but the damage was done. One sin led to another—then led to tragedy. David escaped because of his scheme, but in the process he caused the death of hundreds of innocent people. What a price to pay for disobedience and lack of trust in God!

## David's Third Scheme

Before David learned from his mistakes—before he even learned about the death of the people in Nob—he concocted yet another scheme. This time his behavior was even more bizarre.

David left Nob and headed into enemy territory, hoping he no longer would be recognized as a warrior in Israel. But he was wrong. The servants of Achish, king of Gath, recognized him (21:10–11).

David's anxiety now reached almost unbearable proportions. We're told he "greatly feared Achish" (v. 12). David panicked and feigned madness. In a pathetic portrayal of insanity he "scribbled on the doors of the gate, and let his saliva run down into his beard" (v. 13). Could this be the one God had called "a man after His own heart?"

Again, David's scheme worked—at least he escaped injury. Finding himself in a lonely cave, he began to reflect on his bizarre and sinful behavior. There in the darkness, he once again began to focus his heart and mind on the Lord. He had learned a number of very painful lessons.

## *What Had David Learned?*

We're not told how long it took David to confess his sins and be restored to fellowship with God. However, we know it eventually happened. Psalm 34 speaks volumes, since David probably composed these thoughts while sitting alone in that cave. Read against the backdrop of what we've learned about David's sins, it is self-explanatory.

David focuses back on God and His power—not on himself and his own abilities. He wanted to warn others so they wouldn't make the same mistakes:

### Remain Humble!

> I will bless the *LORD* at all times;
> *His* praise shall continually be in my mouth.
> My soul shall make its boast *in the LORD*;
> The humble shall hear it and rejoice.
> O magnify the *LORD* with me,
> And let us exalt *His name* together.

### Keep Praying!

> I sought the *LORD*, and *He* answered me,
> And delivered me from all my *fears*.
> They looked to *Him* and were radiant,
> And their faces shall never be ashamed.
> This poor man cried and the *LORD* heard him;
> And saved him out of all his troubles.
> The angel of the *LORD* encamps around those who
> *fear Him*,
> And rescues them.

## Trust God!

O taste and see that the *LORD* is good;
How blessed is the man who takes *refuge in Him!*
O fear the *LORD*, you His saints;
For to those who fear *Him*, there is no want.
The young lions do lack and suffer hunger;
But they who seek the *LORD* shall not be in
want of any good thing.

## Be Honest!

Come, you children, listen to me;
*I will teach you the fear of the LORD.*
Who is the man who desires life,
And loves length of days that he may see good?
Keep your tongue from evil,
And your lips from *speaking deceit.*
Depart from evil, and do good;
Seek peace, and pursue it.

## Be Righteous!

The *eyes of the LORD* are toward the righteous,
And His ears are open to their cry.
The *face of the LORD is against evildoers,*
To cut off the memory of them from the earth.
The righteous cry and the *LORD* hears,
And delivers them out of all their troubles.
The *LORD* is near to the brokenhearted,
And saves those who are crushed in spirit.

## Rest in God!

Many are the afflictions of the righteous;
But the *LORD* delivers him out of them all.
He keeps all his bones;
Not one of them is broken.
Evil shall slay the wicked;

And those who hate the righteous will
be condemned.
The *LORD* redeems the soul of His servants;
And none of those who take refuge in Him will
be condemned. (Psalm 34)

## *A Quick Perspective*

During this period in David's life, he was spiritually and emotionally confused. His circumstances and pressures became a maze of bewilderment. He couldn't "see the forest for the trees." Somehow he couldn't seem to remember either God's previous promises or provisions. And even God's immediate care and concern seemed blurred and out of focus. Rather than responding to God's supernatural help by trusting the Lord to help him escape Saul's death traps, David took matters into his own hands. He schemed and connived.

As usually happens in such cases, matters got worse. True, David's schemes helped him escape death. But the ultimate results were tragic:

- Because of his *first scheme,* David and his beloved friend Jonathan were separated, never to see each other again.
- His *second scheme* cost many innocent people their lives and brought guilt into his own life.
- His *third scheme* stands out as a miserable testimony before the pagan king of Gath and his people.

## Becoming God's Man Today

*Principles to Live By*

Have you ever lost perspective, and become unable to remember God's promises and provisions in your own life?

Do even the Lord's daily miracles, such as health and strength, sometimes seem unrelated to the supernatural?

Have you ever taken matters into your own hands and made a mess of things?

At times like these we—like David—hurt those closest to us, cause innocent people to suffer, and bring reproach on the name of Jesus Christ.

It's also at times like these that we begin to allow dishonesty to creep into our lives. Our first scheme may include just a little white lie, but our next step leads to a boldfaced one. Before we know it, we're in so deep we're feigning something we are not. We've moved from telling lies to living them.

Remember these principles

### *Principle 1. Turning to God is always the right choice.*

True, David blew it! He failed God miserably! But David also turned from his sin and once again acknowledged the Lord.

Maybe you too are a man after God's heart, but you've blown it. In a state of anxiety and fear you've taken matters into your own hands. In the process, you've been dishonest and matters have gone from bad to worse. You know you're living out of the will of God.

There's no better time to remember David. In a lonely cave, he came to his senses. He refocused his life. He confessed his sin. And so can you—wherever you find yourself. There is no darkness that God's love and grace cannot penetrate!

Remember that there is forgiveness in Jesus Christ. The Savior has already made atonement for your sins. Believe it, accept it, and appropriate that forgiveness by acknowledging your sin and turning from it. Remember the words of the Apostle John: "If we confess our sins, He is faithful and righteous to forgive us our sins and to cleanse us from all unrighteousness" (1 John 1:9).

### *Principle 2. Trusting God goes hand in hand with our own responsibility.*

Remember that trusting God doesn't mean we are not responsible. When David took on Goliath, he had a plan. But that plan was born in prayer and undergirded by faith. David knew he could do nothing without God's help. Furthermore, at that time David was straightforward and honest. He gave glory and honor to God.

## Becoming a Man after God's Heart

If you have made some decisions as a result of this study, you too may wish to write a "psalm" reflecting the differences in your life, just as David did. If you do, share it with your closest friend!

The following New Testament verses present God's standard for our relationships with others. How does your life measure up? Check yourself! *Underscore any area where you fall short.* Then select one area you've underlined and set a goal. For example, you may underline "do not cause anyone to stumble" because you know this is something you tend to do.

"Therefore each of you must put off falsehood and speak truthfully to his neighbor, for we are all members of one body" (Eph. 4:25, NIV).

"Make it your ambition to lead a quiet life, to mind your own business and to work with your hands, just as we told you, so that your daily life may win the respect of outsiders and so that you will not be dependent on anybody" (1 Thess. 4:11–12, NIV).

"So whether you eat or drink or whatever you do, do it all for the glory of God. Do not cause anyone to stumble, whether Jews, Greeks or the church of God" (1 Cor. 10:31–32, NIV).

"Live such good lives among the pagans that, though they accuse you of doing wrong, they may see your good deeds and glorify God on the day he visits us" (1 Pet. 2:12, NIV).

*Set a Goal*

With God's help, I will begin immediately to carry out the following goal in my life:

________________________________________

________________________________________

________________________________________

________________________________________

## *Memorize the Following Scripture*

***Be wise in the way you act toward outsiders; make the most of every opportunity. Let your conversation be always full of grace, seasoned with salt, so that you may know how to answer everyone.***

COLOSSIANS 4:5–6, NIV

Chapter 8

# *Moving from Fear to Faith*

Read 1 Samuel 23; Psalms 27 and 31

As a relatively young man, I went through a period of deep disillusionment, depression—even despair. The girl I deeply loved suddenly fell ill and, within a matter of months, died. It didn't make sense to me. She was a dedicated Christian. Her parents had been faithful missionaries. "God, where are you?" I asked.

At the same time, several Christian leaders whom I respected developed some serious misunderstandings among themselves, leaving me "caught in the middle." Each ended up confiding in me about the others. I wasn't mature enough as a Christian to handle it. I took my eyes off the Lord Jesus Christ and became very disillusioned. I began to doubt whether or not God heard my prayers. In my deep loneliness I began to doubt the reality of my Christian experience. In fact, I began to doubt whether or not Christianity was real.

## *My Own Dark Cave*

It was in the midst of this "deep, dark cave" in my own life that I began to see why God had allowed it all to happen. I needed to learn an important lesson: no matter how others fail

God, no matter what crises come in life—Jesus Christ never changes. He is the same yesterday, today, and forever.

I also saw that God was dealing with other weaknesses in my life—specifically prejudice and self-righteousness. All of this was a part of His plan to prepare me for future ministry. I eventually emerged from the experience a different man.

My disillusionment became a turning point in my life. Though I've gone through the normal struggles regarding my relationship with God, I've never been the same since. I've never doubted the reality of Christianity—that Jesus Christ is the Son of God and that He is truly my Lord and Savior. I hope I never will!

Following David's period of darkness and fear—which caused him to take matters into his own hands and make a woeful mess of things—he also emerged from the cave of Adullam a different man. While hiding from Saul, he had many quiet hours to think and reflect on his bizarre and deceitful behavior. In the silent darkness, he had a close encounter with his Lord. God had his undivided attention.

## *When the Sun Shines Again*

The dark cave of Adullam was a much different environment from the hillsides of Judea where David cared for his father's sheep and enjoyed an intimate relationship with his Maker. But it provided an aura in which to grasp the darkness that had captured his own soul. Once again the light of God's revelation brightened his outlook on life and brought him a sense of inner security. The sunlight of God's love and care diffused his profound fear and refocused his bizarre thoughts. David once again trusted God rather than relying on his own skills and abilities. And once again he faced his problems with a divine perspective.

### Again—the Man He Once Was

Sometime soon after David's thinking cleared, he received word that the Philistines had attacked Israel at Keilah (1 Sam. 23:1).

David's reaction reflects the man he once was! This was the man who had amazed and thrilled the hearts of his people—the David who faced the lion and the bear with great confidence in God, the David who slew Goliath and won many victories over the Philistines.

We see the greatest reflection of the "man David once was" when he "inquired of the LORD, saying, 'Shall I go and attack these Philistines?'" God responded to David's prayer: "Go and attack the Philistines, and deliver Keilah" (v. 2).

## David's Motley Crew

David's four hundred men recoiled from this challenge with tremendous hesitation and fear. "Behold," they said, "we are afraid here in Judah. How much more then if we go to Keilah against the ranks of the Philistines?" (v. 3).

From a human perspective, we can understand why these men were so fearful. First, they weren't first-class soldiers. In fact, their classification could be "3-D." Scripture records that "everyone who was in *distress*, and everyone who was in *debt*, and everyone who was *discontented*, gathered to" join David in the cave of Adullam (22:2).

What a nucleus for an army! They were a motley crew—outlaws, if you will—on the run because of their rebellion against Saul's government. They were men who owed others money, and were unable—or unwilling—to pay it back. They were men whose hearts were already embittered and angry because of what they felt were injustices in their society.

## You Must Be Crazy!

When David issued an order to attack the Philistine army in Keilah, their fear went through the roof! Though they probably never voiced it—at least to David—they must have thought he was out of his mind. Remember too that these men were few in number and ill-equipped. Any competent military strategist would have told them they were loony to attack the well-armed and well-trained Philistines.

## When You're Feeling Down, Look Up!

David's response discloses how well he had learned his lesson. *Fear begets fear,* especially in those who are already anxious. Had David not regained his spiritual and emotional bearings, he would have regressed and succumbed. He may have had "flashbacks" of his previous obsessions and fears, but rather than being pulled down by his men's pessimism, David *looked up to the Lord.* We read, "Then David inquired of the LORD once more. And, the LORD answered him and said, 'Arise, go down to Keilah, for I will give the Philistines into your hand'" (23:4).

Reassured by God's promises, David boldly led his men to Keilah and delivered his fellow Israelites from the Philistines. He had moved from fear to faith. The hand of God was upon David as before. Once again he was functioning with a divine perspective in solving life's problems.

## Saul Was Still on the Prowl

Saul continued to track David. Word soon got back to the king that David was in Keilah. Immediately, Saul commissioned his soldiers "to go down to Keilah to besiege David and his men" (v. 8).

David's renewed faith was not only revealed in his dealings with the Philistines, but also in his relationship with Saul. As soon as he heard about the king's plot, he once again consulted the Lord, asking some very specific questions: "O LORD God of Israel, Thy servant has heard for certain that Saul is seeking to come to Keilah to destroy the city on my account. Will the men of Keilah surrender me into his hand? Will Saul come down just as Thy servant has heard? O LORD God of Israel, I pray, tell Thy servant" (vv. 10–12).

David's prayer indicates his reliance on God. He didn't want to act on man's word alone. What he heard may or may not have been true. Furthermore, God had thwarted some of Saul's previous attempts on his life. David wanted to know for sure if Saul would indeed come to Keilah and what would happen there.

## Specific Questions—Specific Answers

God answered David's prayer. David had asked specific questions and he got a specific answer. We read, "And the LORD said, 'He will come down'" (v. 11).

But if you compare God's response to David's queries, you'll note that the Lord answered David's second question but not his first. So David asked the first question again. He clearly wanted to know what would actually happen if he remained inside the walls of the city. Thus David restated his question, "Will the men of Keilah surrender me and my men into the hands of Saul?" Again the Lord's answer was specific: "They will surrender you" (v. 12).

David and his men were in danger. Now numbering about six hundred, they fled Keilah. When word got back to Saul that David and his army had left the city, he changed his mind and halted his attack.

## Not to Be Denied!

But Saul would not give up. He hardened his heart even more. He was determined to take David's life. So, he continued his angry search. But all his efforts were to no avail. As long as David trusted the Lord and sought His will and guidance, he continually escaped from Saul's death traps. Thus Saul "sought him every day, but God did not deliver him into his hand" (v. 14).

# *David's Journal*

During this renewal period of faith and confidence in God, David recorded his thoughts. Inspired by the Holy Spirit, he composed Psalms 27 and 31, which certainly speak of his new perspective. Read, meditate, and reflect on the opening lines in each of these psalms:

## Whom Shall I Fear? Whom Shall I Dread?

> The LORD is my light and my salvation;
> Whom shall I fear?

The LORD is the defense of my life;
Whom shall I dread?
When evildoers came upon me to devour my flesh,
My adversaries and my enemies, they stumbled
and fell.
Though a host encamp against me,
My heart will not fear;
Though war arise against me,
In spite of this I shall be confident. (27:1–3)

## "Thou Art My Rock . . . My Fortress . . . My Strength"

In Thee, O LORD, I have taken refuge;
Let me never be ashamed;
In Thy righteousness deliver me.
Incline Thine ear to me, rescue me quickly;
Be Thou to me a rock of strength,
A stronghold to save me.
For Thou art my rock and my fortress;
For Thy name's sake Thou wilt lead me
and guide me.
Thou wilt pull me out of the net which they have
secretly laid for me;
For Thou art my strength.
Into Thy hand I commit my spirit;
Thou hast ransomed me, O LORD, God of truth. (31:1–5)

## Becoming God's Man Today

*Principles to Live By*

As a Christian man, can you identify with David? We all face fears and failures—and challenges that seem beyond our abilities to handle. How can we learn to trust God in the midst of these desperate situations? How can we develop a divine perspective on life—in our marriages, our families, our jobs, and in our personal trials and temptations?

### *Principle 1. We must learn from our mistakes.*

This was one of David's secrets.

1. Rather than allowing his failures to hold him captive, he turned to God.

2. Rather than wallowing in self-pity, he turned his eyes heavenward.

3. Rather than repeating old patterns, he refocused his attitudes and behavior.

*What About You?*

1. Are you learning from past mistakes, or are you repeating them?

2. Do you have a tendency to introspect and feel sorry for yourself rather than thinking of God's blessings?

3. Are you locked into the past, or are you allowing God to break the shackles of failure that have bound you?

*Remember God's Promises*

The Lord wants to be your light and your salvation—just as He was David's. He will be the defense of your life. You need not fear. Trust Him! Step out in faith believing that He will be your source of strength no matter what the problem.

### *Principle 2. We must seek His will through His Word.*

One very significant lesson David learned was that he couldn't solve his problems by himself. He needed God's wisdom—and so do you and I!

In difficult days God often spoke directly to some of His key leaders. David had direct access to God. He actually conversed with the Lord, as did Moses and Abraham.

Today God speaks to us through the Bible. We have His Word. In the Scriptures He reveals His will for all mankind. Furthermore, it is through His Word that we develop faith. This is why Paul wrote, "Faith comes from hearing the message, and the message is heard through the word of Christ" (Rom. 10:17, NIV).

*What About You?*

1. How consistent are you in learning more and more of His Word? As you do, you will learn more and more of His will in all aspects of your life.

2. Are you studying the Word regularly, preferably daily?

3. Do you consult the Scriptures when you face problems?

4. Do you search God's Word when you are making important decisions?

*Remember God's Words to Joshua*

> "This book of the law shall not depart from your mouth, but you shall meditate on it day and night, so that you may be careful to do according to all that is written in it; for then you will make your way prosperous, and then you will have success." (Joshua 1:8)

## *Principle 3. We must seek His will through prayer.*

David did not hesitate to ask God specific questions. When he did, he got specific answers. Though God does not speak directly to His children as often as He did with certain leaders of old, He does answer prayer. He speaks through His revealed Word. He enlightens us through circumstances. And He gives us wisdom through other members of the Body of Christ.

*Divine Wisdom*

Though God normally speaks through the Scriptures, we must also remember His words to James—which are perhaps even more relevant to David's situation and example:

> Consider it pure joy, my brothers, whenever you face trials of many kinds, because you know that the testing of your faith develops perseverance. Perseverance must finish its work so that you may be mature and complete, not lacking anything. *If any of you lacks wisdom, he should ask God,* who gives generously to all without finding fault, and it will be given to him. But when he asks he must believe and not doubt, because he who doubts is like a wave of the sea, blown and tossed by the wind. That man

should not think he will receive anything from the Lord; he is a double-minded man, unstable in all he does. (James 1:2–8, NIV)

### *Principle 4. We must develop our faith through relationships with other Christians.*

Fear begets fear! But faith begets faith!

1. If you want to be fearful, associate with people who are fearful.

2. If you want to be pessimistic, associate with people who are pessimistic.

3. If you want to learn to trust God, associate with people who trust God.

#### *A Well-Known "Secret"*

This is a well-known principle. I've experienced it in my own spiritual experience—as I'm sure you have. This process has become particularly meaningful to me—especially as a pastor—as I have begun participating more fully in the "body life" of the churches I have led.

True, the Word of God is basic in producing faith and trust in God. But learning what God says can easily become abstract truth that doesn't really affect our attitudes and actions. The greatest impact in my own life of faith comes when I see God's truth fleshed out in the lives of other believers. I learn best:

1. When I observe other Christians learning from their past mistakes.

2. When I see brothers and sisters in Christ applying God's Word in their own lives.

3. When I see fellow believers praying in faith and receiving answers to prayer.

It's then that:

1. I sense my own faith growing and developing.

2. My own spiritual perspectives broaden and deepen.

3. My own personal Christianity takes on new meaning and hope.

*My Own "Weekend" Experiences*

For years I have participated in leading multiple worship services on the weekend. Some might call these "*weak end*" responsibilities.

Not so! When people ask me how I can handle this responsibility physically and emotionally, I give a simple answer: I am buoyed spiritually by observing what God is doing in the lives of other members of the Body of Christ. When I see God at work in the lives of other believers, it strengthens my own faith. It encourages me to trust God personally. I see Christianity at work. These experiences actually give me psychological and physical energy.

My experience should not be surprising. The Word of God teaches that we all need to learn the Word of God and have dynamic and vital relationships experiences with each other in order to grow spiritually. In the words of Paul, "From him [Christ] the whole body, joined and held together by every supporting ligament, grows and builds itself up in love, as each part does its work" (Eph. 4:16, NIV).

*Consider Also These Powerful Proverbs*

- "Anxiety in the heart of a man weighs it down, but a good word makes it glad" (12:25).
- "Pleasant words are a honeycomb, sweet to the soul and healing to the bones" (16:24).
- "A joyful heart is good medicine, but a broken spirit dries up the bones" (17:22).
- "Like apples of gold in settings of silver is a word spoken in right circumstances" (25:11).

## Becoming a Man after God's Heart

What are you doing to develop a divine perspective in your Christian life? In what areas are you strong? In what areas do you need strengthening? What can you do right now to be more obedient in carrying out God's will for your life?

*Check Yourself!*

As you evaluate your life in view of the following principles, ask the Holy Spirit to impress on your heart one lesson you need to apply more effectively in your life. Then write out a specific goal. For example, perhaps you seldom learn from your past mistakes; you may keep repeating them in some form or fashion.

1. I am learning from my past mistakes:
   ____ seldom ____ sometimes ____ most of the time;

2. I am seeking God's will:
   ➢ Through learning His Word
   ____ seldom ____ sometimes ____ most of the time;
   ➢ Through regular private reading and study
   ____ seldom ____ sometimes ____ most of the time;
   ➢ Through regular exposure to public teaching of the Word
   ____ seldom ____ sometimes ____ most of the time;

3. I am regularly participating in the life of my church and entering into the following experiences with other Christians:
   ➢ Identifying the needs of others
   ____ seldom ____ sometimes ____ most of the time;
   ➢ Praying for the needs of others
   ____ seldom ____ sometimes ____ most of the time;
   ➢ Encouraging others
   ____ seldom ____ sometimes ____ most of the time;
   ➢ Honoring others
   ____ seldom ____ sometimes ____ most of the time;
   ➢ Greeting and welcoming others
   ____ seldom ____ sometimes ____ most of the time;

➢ Serving others

____ seldom ____ sometimes ____ most of the time;

➢ Bearing the burdens of others

____ seldom ____ sometimes ____ most of the time;

➢ Sharing my concern and consecrated interest in others with my presence

____ seldom ____ sometimes ____ most of the time;

### *Set a Goal*

With God's help, I will begin immediately to carry out the following goal in my life:

______________________________________________

______________________________________________

______________________________________________

______________________________________________

### *Memorize the Following Scripture*

> ***Do not be anxious about anything, but in everything, by prayer and petition, with thanksgiving, present your requests to God. And the peace of God, which transcends all understanding, will guard your hearts and your minds in Christ Jesus.***
>
> PHILIPPIANS 4:6–7, NIV

Chapter 9

# *A Man Who Loved His Enemy*

Read 1 Samuel 24:1–22; 26:1–25

*I*'ve known very few people in my life I'd call enemies. However, as I thought about David's experience, I didn't have to reflect long about personal relationships over the years before remembering one man who claimed to be a Christian but who turned out to be an "enemy." Some identified him as a "wolf in sheep's clothing," although I have sincerely attempted not to pass judgment on his personal relationship with God. I would not be surprised, however, to discover someday that he is—at least at this point—not a born-again Christian. From my personal experience, I've seen little evidence of fruit in his life.

## *A Personal Struggle*

I would not be honest if I didn't admit that I went through a difficult period when I found it very hard to love this man in the true biblical sense. I knew he had moral failures in his life and was persistently dishonest—two sins that are constant "bedfellows."

There were times when I could see clearly that this man was continuing to deceive others as he had deceived me. I was tempted to expose his sins. I sought counsel from others who knew the situation, and they wisely advised me not to pursue the matter. But, I must admit I had some serious talks with God about why He had not disciplined this man.

God *did* deal with this man—but in His own time. If I had been involved my actions may have been driven by a desire to "get even"—or as Paul said, "pay back evil for evil"—which a Christian should never do! (Rom. 12:17)

I'm not suggesting a Christian can't confront sin. That's part of our God-given responsibility (Gal. 6:1–2). But I and many others had tried with no success in this man's case. But in time his sin was revealed. God used others to confront him, with more evidence than I had. I'm convinced it was God's timing. By evaluating my own motives, I was able to "overcome evil with good" (Rom. 12:21).

## *David's Powerful Example*

Two events in the life of David dramatically demonstrate his sensitivity toward God and man. Both incidents involved encounters with Saul, and both provided David with an opportunity to take Saul's life. In each instance, however, David did the right thing—even though he faced unusual temptation. He showed love to the man who hated him. David became a dynamic model to all of us who are tempted to retaliate by hurting someone who has hurt us—and who may be continuing to hurt us.

### God's Providential Care

David miraculously continued to escape Saul's death traps. Once he was betrayed by the Ziphites. Saul and his army surrounded David and his small band of men (1 Sam. 23:26). There was no way of escape. But just when it seemed that it was all over for David, the Philistines invaded Israel and Saul had to give up his attack in order to pursue his larger interests. Once again, God sovereignly protected David.

## David's Hiding Place

What happened next is ironic. David and his little band took refuge "in the wilderness of Engedi"—a place designated as the "Rocks of the Wild Goats" (24:1–2). There were dozens of caverns and caves in this area—one so large that it once sheltered thirty thousand people from a terrible storm. Many believe this was the cave David used as a hiding place from Saul.

## Saul's Determination

After his battle with the Philistines, Saul once again discovered David's general location. And once again he pursued David—taking three thousand of his best warriors with him. Saul's behavior demonstrates vividly how bitterness can twist a man's soul. His heart was hard and his ears were deaf to God's sovereign will.

If it weren't so pathetic, what happened next would be almost humorous. While searching for David, Saul took refuge from the hot sun in the very cave where David and his men were hiding. Lurking in the shadows, they were invisible to Saul. He thought he was alone.

David's men were overjoyed; here was David's golden opportunity. In fact, they actually interpreted what was happening as the Lord's provision. Thus they said to David, "Behold, this is the day of which the Lord said to you, 'Behold; I am about to give your enemy into your hand, and you shall do to him as it seems good to you'" (v. 4).

Apparently, David's men were paraphrasing some of his psalms. Perhaps they were referring to their previous experience in the cave of Adullam when David had written, "The face of the LORD is against evildoers, to cut off the memory of them from the earth" (Ps. 34:16). It's not surprising that they saw in this present "cave experience" a grand opportunity to help the Lord eliminate David's greatest foe.

As David watched Saul sleeping, he must have remembered the times Saul had tried to pin him to the wall with his spear. He must have thought of the times the king had sent him into battle against the Philistines hoping he would be killed. And how could he forget the times Saul had nearly captured him with his well-trained army?

What an opportunity to avenge himself! The temptation was great—and David seemingly took some initial steps to carry out what appeared to be an opportunity from the Lord Himself to put an end once and for all to this struggle.

To draw this conclusion, we have to read between the lines. Apparently Saul fell asleep in the coolness of the cave. While he dozed, David must have crept up on Saul and "cut off the edge" of his robe. However, David immediately felt guilty. We read that his "conscience bothered him" (1 Sam. 24:4–5).

There must have been something in David's heart—something about his motives—that troubled him deeply about what appears to be a harmless act. Had he actually contemplated killing Saul? Or was his heart simply filled with pride, choosing a symbolic way to demonstrate to his men that he eventually would be the king of Israel? Perhaps he was simply going to taunt Saul as he allowed his men to capture and kill him.

Whatever David's motive, he felt guilt-stricken. If he had a scheme in mind, he quickly confessed his error to his men and persuaded them not to harm the king (v. 7).

## David's Act of Humility

When Saul awakened and left the cave, David followed and called after him. With sincere humility and deep respect, he pleaded with Saul, "Why do you listen to the words of men, saying, 'Behold, David seeks to harm you'"? (v. 9) To demonstrate his own pure motives, he held up the piece of Saul's robe, proving that he had no intention of killing him.

## Saul's Confession

Saul knew instantly what had happened. David had an opportunity to kill him but had spared his life. There was no way he could misconstrue the facts. Looking at his robe and the missing piece, he knew David could have severed his head with one stroke. He was humbled. He wept before David and confessed his wickedness. He acknowledged that God had delivered him into David's hands, and yet David had not killed him.

For a moment, we see a man moved to tears. Saul was overwhelmed with David's mercy. "If a man finds his enemy, will he let him go away safely?" queried Saul. "May the LORD therefore reward you with good in return for what you have done to me this day" (v. 19).

As far as we know, this is the first time Saul confessed publicly that he knew in his heart that David was going to be the king of Israel. He only pleaded that when this happened, David would spare his life, his descendants and his relatives (vv. 20–21).

### David's Skepticism

David promised to protect Saul and his extended family. But he knew instinctively that the king's repentance was not total. If it had been, Saul would have turned over his royal robe that very day and anointed David king in his place. Rather, Saul turned and went back to his throne and David and his men went on to find another place where they could live in safety.

David's assessment was correct. Yet again Saul changed his attitude toward David and pursued him. How quickly we can forget God's mercy and grace and revert to our old behavior!

## *Saul's Repeat Performance*

Anyone reading the story of David's life and his association with King Saul, even for the first time, could easily predict what was going to happen next.

Just as he had done so many times before, Saul reverted to his old patterns of behavior. Jealousy and anger once again possessed him. He went on another rampage, trying to find David and kill him.

As before, the Ziphites—seeking to gain some prestige and position with the king of Israel—informed Saul of David's general location. Saul once again put together an army of three thousand of his best men and began to search for David in the wilderness of Ziph.

## David's Midnight Appearance

Events in this story are similar to Saul's earlier attempt to capture David—yet distinctive. Anticipating Saul's change of heart, David had his own men on the lookout. He soon got word Saul was on his way.

Rather than waiting for Saul to find him, David discovered the king's exact location and decided to make a "midnight appearance." While Saul and his army were asleep, David and one of his men, Abishai, crept undetected into Saul's camp. Once again the Lord was with David; He caused a deep sleep to come upon Saul and his company of soldiers. Even Abner, Saul's chief bodyguard, was fast asleep (26:12).

## Another Golden Opportunity

Abishai, sensing another golden opportunity to deal with Saul once and for all, begged David to let him kill the king. But once again David protected Saul. Rather than harming him, the two took his spear and a jug of water beside his head and left the camp. They descended into the valley and climbed up another mountain. From there David called—not to Saul—but to Abner, chiding him for allowing the king to go unattended and unprotected.

As David called out to Abner, he taught the king a lesson —even though he was directing his words at his chief bodyguard: "Are you not a man? And who is like you in Israel? Why then have you not guarded your lord the king? For one of the people came to destroy the king your lord. This thing that you have done is not good. As the LORD lives, all of you must surely die, because you did not guard your lord, the LORD'S anointed. And now, see where the king's spear is, and the jug of water that was at his head" (vv. 15–16).

There stood David with Saul's spear. How easy it would have been to plunge it into Saul's heart! At one time, David had served as a better bodyguard to Saul than Abner. More importantly, David made it clear that someone so careless in guarding the king should die. In other words, David was making it very clear that it was totally irrational for Saul to seek his life when those who were on Saul's side weren't as concerned for his life as David was.

## Broken Promises Take Their Toll

As before, Saul realized he was falsely judging David. He invited David to come with him—*promising* never to attempt to take his life again. David, however, could no longer trust the king. He returned Saul's spear but turned and walked away. David knew he could never be safe in Saul's presence. But he also knew he had conveyed to the king his own pure motives. His conscience was clear, but he would have to live as a fugitive until the Lord Himself removed Saul.

## Becoming God's Man Today

*Principles to Live By*

Think for a moment about what happened. How easily David could have interpreted these opportunities to take Saul's life as chances provided by the Lord Himself. How easy it would have been to rationalize, particularly since David knew it was God's plan for him to replace Saul as king. From a human point of view, David could have positioned himself as victor and every soldier in Israel would have rallied to support him—especially since they were well-aware of Saul's unpredictable personality and inconsistent behavior.

David, however, did not yield to those tempting thoughts. He knew it wouldn't be right for him to take matters into his own hands and harm Saul.

As Christian men, we can learn some dynamic lessons from this experience in David's life.

### *Principle 1. Contentious Christian brothers are not ordinary enemies.*

David recognized Saul was anointed by God. He was no ordinary enemy. In the same way, Christian brothers who may be troubling us in some way are not ordinary enemies either. They may be out to hurt us, their motives may be selfish and they may be vindictive. But this doesn't entitle any of us to return evil for evil to another Christian. A believer is not to return evil for evil to *anyone.* Jesus Himself set this standard when He said:

> You have heard that it was said, 'Love your neighbor and hate your enemy.' But I tell you: Love your enemies and pray for those who persecute you, that you may be sons of your Father in heaven. He causes his sun to rise on the evil and the good, and sends rain on the righteous and the unrighteous. If you love those who love you, what reward will you get? Are not even the tax collectors doing that? And if you greet only your brothers, what are you doing more than others? Do not even pagans do that? Be perfect, therefore, as your heavenly Father is perfect. (Matt. 5:43–48, NIV)

### *Principle 2. A conscience that is in tune with God's Word is a great asset.*

David developed a sensitive conscience that was in tune with the will of God. As men, we can learn from David's experience. We must be on guard against allowing ourselves to "compartmentalize" our values.

Sadly, some Christian men live double lives, seemingly without any regrets. They live one way when they're at home and in church and another way when they set foot in the business world. Facing the demands of the job, they gradually allow their consciences to become seared. They find themselves lying, stealing, using foul language, and treating others with disdain—just like their secular counterparts.

To be men after God's heart, we must never allow this to happen. And if it has, we must take steps immediately to overcome this kind of duplicity. Our conscience is a very important part of our total being. It's critical that we keep it constantly in tune with the Word of God.

### *Is It Possible to be Overly Conscientious?*

The answer is a decided "yes!" Some men develop an over-sensitive conscience—one that is tuned to man's will rather than God's. For example, I used to feel guilty about things for which I never should have felt guilty. My conscience was tuned to man-made rules and regulations rather than God's. I even felt guilty about associating with other Christians outside of my particular church environment. This is what I'd been taught for years. It took time for me to re-tune my conscience to God's will rather than what I had been falsely taught.

The greater problem among Christians, however, is to see a man develop an *insensitive* conscience that is out of harmony with God's will. Paul refers to people like this when he states that their "consciences have been seared as with a hot iron" (1 Tim. 4:2, NIV).

At this moment in his life, David had a balance. His conscience was sensitive, but not over-sensitive. He knew what was right and wrong because of his personal relationship with God and his knowledge of the Word of God. In this instance, he knew it would be absolutely wrong to take Saul's life, even though his own men felt he had a perfect right to do so.

### *Principle 3. We must be on guard against reaching a "point of no return" when walking out of the will of God.*

Though David was tempted to return evil for evil, he checked his behavior before he made an irreversible decision that would have haunted him the rest of his life. All of us are tempted to do wrong, especially when someone treats us badly. When this happens, most of us react emotionally and defensively and begin to move in the direction of doing wrong before we gain a proper spiritual perspective.

The important lesson from David's life is that we stop ourselves before we do something we cannot correct. We must remember that in the "heat of the moment," we are the most vulnerable. Once we move in the direction of being vindictive, it's easy to go all the way. Not so with David. Even under extreme pressure from his own men, he confessed his improper motives and turned away from doing what was wrong. And this leads to another important principle.

### *Principle 4. Social pressure can lead to devastating decisions.*

In both situations we've looked at in this chapter, David was encouraged by others to vindicate himself by taking Saul's life (1 Sam. 24:4; 26:8). How easy it would have been for him to take their advice. Some of his most trusted men believed revenge was the right thing to do. David demonstrated true character when he stood strong against the tide of opinion. He knew harming Saul would be wrong—period. He held fast to his convictions.

### *Principle 5. It's not wrong for Christians to defend themselves when they're being mistreated, but we must do so with a proper attitude.*

There is no question that David had a right to defend himself against Saul. But he responded with true humility and deep respect.

Some Christians believe they have no rights. This is not true. David had a perfect right to defend himself. But he did so in a proper way. He simply confronted Saul with the facts. He also demonstrated his loyalty. But as he did, he shared his inner feelings of frustration and stress. He actually pleaded with Saul to understand.

There are times, of course, when we must "turn the other cheek." But this doesn't mean it's wrong to defend ourselves when we have been falsely accused. The Apostle Paul demonstrates this dramatically in his letter to the Corinthians. When he was falsely accused, he set the record straight (1 Cor. 9:1–27). But it's wrong to retaliate and get even. There is a difference! And this leads us to yet another principle.

### *Principle 6. God is the only One who has the ultimate right to punish those who have hurt us.*

In both encounters we looked at, David made this point very obvious. During the first confrontation, David said, "May the LORD judge between you and me, and may the LORD avenge me on you; but my hand shall not be against you. . . . The LORD therefore be judge and decide between you and me; and may He see and plead my cause, and deliver me from your hand" (1 Sam. 24:12,15).

During the second encounter, David also said to Abishai—who wanted to take Saul's life—"As the LORD lives, surely the LORD will strike him, or his day will come that he dies, or he will go down into battle and perish" (26:10).

Paul summarized God's will for Christians in situations like this when he wrote to the Romans:

> Do not repay anyone evil for evil. Be careful to do what is right in the eyes of everybody. If it is possible, as far as it depends on you, live at peace with everyone. Do not take revenge, my friends, but leave room for God's wrath, for it is written: "It is mine to avenge; I will repay," says the Lord. On the contrary: "If your enemy is hungry, feed him; if he is thirsty, give him something to drink. In doing this, you will heap burning coals on his head." Do not be overcome by evil, but overcome evil with good. (Rom. 12:17–21, NIV)

It's important to understand that the principle of forgiveness so prevalent in the Bible does not give criminals permission to hurt others. God has set a very high standard for those who are "governing authorities." Those who live by the sword are to die by the sword. However, this is a responsibility God has delegated to civil authorities—men and women who are to make sure the rights of people are protected in any society.

### *Principle 7. When we've forgiven others and do not retaliate, it does not necessarily mean we can have a trusting relationship.*

Though David followed God's principles in dealing with Saul in these two instances, he realized he could never fully trust the king again. This is apparent from David's behavior—and understandably so. When Saul invited David to come and be in his presence following the second encounter, David's reply was kind but negative. He had made his point with Saul—he did not return evil for evil—but he could not entrust his life to the king. Consequently, "David went on his way, and Saul returned to his place" (1 Sam. 26:25).

As Christians, we must forgive one another. I believe we are to also do everything we can to re-establish trust, even going the extra mile in reaching out to our enemies. However, there are times when it is no longer possible to trust another person totally. Like Saul, some people demonstrate again and again their untrustworthiness and unpredictable behavior.

Following David's second encounter with Saul, his final words were very insightful: "Now behold, as your life was highly valued in my sight this day, so may my life be highly valued in the sight of the LORD, and may He deliver me from all distress" (v. 26:24).

With these concluding words, David was saying he would never take Saul's life. However, he also was saying that the only one who could ultimately protect his life from Saul was the Lord. Never again would he trust the king.

## Becoming a Man after God's Heart

It is easy to rationalize in our own hearts that another person cannot be trusted. Before we take this course of action, we should review David's numerous attempts to trust Saul before he took his final course of action.

Think of one person in your life who has repeatedly tried to hurt you. The following questions are designed to help you use David's example to evaluate your attitudes and actions toward that individual. Select one area that you feel you need to make a priority in becoming the man you know God wants you to become. Then set a goal. For example, when you are wronged and defend yourself, you may do so with arrogance and anger rather than humility and respect.

1. Have I done all I can to approach this person on a spiritual basis, realizing they too are made in the image of God?

2. In my relationship with this person, is my conscience tuned to the will and Word of God, not to what I want to do to the person?

3. When I am tempted to return evil for evil to this person, do I check my behavior before I've done something irreversible and damaging to my personal testimony?

4. Do I refuse to go along with the crowd in my attitudes and actions toward this unlovable person?

5. When I'm wronged and defend myself, do I do so with humility and respect?

6. Do my attitudes and actions toward this person reflect the fact that I believe God will ultimately make things right—even if I cannot?

7. Have I allowed mistrust to become a part of my behavior prematurely?

*Set a Goal*

With God's help, I will begin immediately to carry out the following goal in my life:

________________________________________

________________________________________

________________________________________

________________________________________

*Memorize the Following Scripture*

*If possible, so far as it depends on you, be at peace with all men. Never take your own revenge, beloved, but leave room for the wrath of God, for it is written, "Vengeance is Mine, I will repay," says the Lord."*

ROMANS 12:18–19

## Chapter 10

# *David's Wounded Ego*

Read 1 Samuel 25

Great leaders often have great weaknesses! History is filled with illustrations, from Roman emperors to U.S. presidents. Unfortunately, this is true not just of pagan and secular leaders but also of men with a great passion for God.

It certainly was true of David. At times he demonstrated great faith; at times he was paralyzed with fear. He "turned the other cheek" toward Saul when the king tried to take his life. When Nabal refused David's request for help, however, David lost his temper because he was rejected by a fool. He became so angry he almost murdered a number of innocent men—all because of a wounded ego.

How ironic! David's patience toward Saul is almost beyond comprehension. If anyone had given him reason to "lose his cool," Saul had. But his reactions to Nabal are just as incomprehensible. He allowed a "fool's" behavior to make him so angry he was determined to retaliate with the sword.

## *A Subtle Enemy*

Following David's encounter with Saul in the dark cave in the wilderness of Engedi, Samuel—God's faithful prophet—died.

David and his men then headed south to the wilderness of Paran. It was here that the children of Israel wandered for many years before entering the land of Canaan.

For a time at least, David felt safe from his enemy, King Saul. But it was here that David encountered a much more subtle enemy—a man named Nabal—which literally means "fool."

Nabal could very well have been in the mind of Jesus when He told the parable of the rich man who was filled with greed and kept building bigger barns to store up his worldly goods. It was then that "God said to him, 'You fool! This very night your life will be demanded from you. Then who will get what you have prepared for yourself?'" (Luke 12:20 NIV).

Nabal also was a fool! His story holds spiritual lessons for all of us. However, let's focus on David and his reactions to Nabal. Perhaps this speaks more loudly to every Christian man than Nabal's behavior. After all, David claimed to be a follower of God. We cannot say the same of Nabal.

Nabal was a rich man. "He had three thousand sheep and a thousand goats" (1 Sam. 25:2). One of his greatest assets was a beautiful and intelligent wife named Abigail who—unlike her husband—was a very sensitive and unselfish person.

Nabal had one goal in life: to store up treasures on this earth. "Eat, drink and be merry" was the story of his life. Unfortunately, he forgot the rest of this ancient one-liner—"for tomorrow we die!" Nabal had not anticipated that prospect. Death was the farthest thing from his mind.

## *Shepherd to Shepherd*

For many days David's men had lived in the same area where Nabal's shepherds grazed his sheep. In fact, they had often protected these men and their animals from harm and danger. Later in our story, one of Nabal's own shepherds painted this beautiful word picture: "The men were very good to us, and we were not insulted, nor did we miss anything as long as we went about with them, while we were in the fields. They were a wall to us both by night and by day, all the time we were with them tending the sheep" (vv. 15–16).

David understood the life of a shepherd. He could identify with the challenges these men face day after day and night after night. Perhaps he saw himself as a "shepherd of shepherds," utilizing his resources to help them do their job.

However, David had another goal in mind. He was responsible for the welfare of six hundred men. He needed food for their hungry stomachs and clothes for their backs. No doubt David anticipated that if he helped these shepherds, their master Nabal would reciprocate.

The time came when Nabal was ready to cash in on his investments. It was "sheep shearing" time in Carmel (v. 2). For most people this was a season to share material blessings with others. Knowing this, David sent ten of his men to talk with Nabal about the need for food and clothing to take care of his army. After all, they had treated Nabal well, helping to guard his flocks and protecting his shepherds. David's request for help was logical and reasonable. Any man with Nabal's resources—and an ounce of common sense—would have responded positively and graciously.

## *David's Greeting and Blessing*

David seemed confident he would get help from Nabal. You can sense it in his message when he told his men to "Go up to Carmel" and "visit Nabal."

Any time we allow someone to use our name to receive a special favor, we're usually quite sure of a positive response. After all, everyone in this area knew about David and his great exploits—from killing the giant Goliath to outwitting Saul.

Nabal's response devastated David's ego. When his men asked for help, they—and David—were totally unprepared for Nabal's reaction. He hurled the greatest insult at David any man could ever give another. "Who is David?" he asked. "And who is the son of Jesse?" (v. 10).

To refuse to share his material blessings was insult enough in light of what David had done for him. But for Nabal actually to deny that he knew David and to classify him as a runaway slave was a horrible snub and put-down. When David received this report, he was infuriated. Overcome with anger, he grabbed his sword and ordered four hundred other men to do the same. There and then he vowed he would kill every man associated with Nabal—which no doubt included Nabal himself (v. 13).

Fortunately, Nabal had a wife who was his opposite. Abigail was wise, discerning, and generous. Her reputation was well-known among Nabal's servants. One of these men was perceptive enough to predict what was going to happen when he observed the way Nabal treated David's men. Knowing that Abigail also would quickly grasp what was about to transpire, the servant lost no time finding her and telling her the whole story.

Unlike her husband, Abigail was no fool! Without consulting her husband, she quickly prepared a "truckload" of food and when out to meet David. She approached him and humbly fell at his feet, taking the blame for her husband's irresponsible actions. Begging for mercy, she minced no words in describing her worthless husband (vv. 24–25).

Just as quickly as David lost control of his emotions, he regained perspective. He saw what he was about to do. His heart was touched and humbled by this woman's openness and honesty. More importantly, he recognized God's hand in what was happening. "Blessed be the Lord God of Israel," David said, "who sent you this day to meet me, and blessed be your discernment, and blessed be you, who have kept me this day from bloodshed, and from avenging myself by my own hand" (vv. 32–33).

## *An Ironic Ending*

After David received Abigail's gift of food, he sent her on her way in peace. When she returned home, she discovered that

Nabal had "over-celebrated" on this festive occasion. Rejoicing in his good fortune, he became so drunk that he was incapable of carrying on an intelligent conversation.

Come morning, when he was sober, Abigail was just as honest with her husband as she had been with David. She told him what had happened.

We're not told what Nabal's emotional reactions were. He was either so filled with anger or fear, or both, that he had a stroke. The text is graphic: "His heart died within him so that he became as a stone" (v. 37). He never recovered. In ten days, he was dead. Doctors today would label his demise as accidental, but the Scriptures make it very clear that God's hand of judgment fell on this wicked and selfish man (v. 38).

## *David's Gesture of Love*

The final scene in this dramatic story is even more ironic. When David heard about Nabal's death, he sent a proposal to Abigail and asked her to become his wife. Apparently it didn't take much thought on her part to accept. Nabal not only lost his life, but also his wife, who married the man he refused to help!

## Becoming God's Man Today

*Principles to Live By*

### *Principle 1. Failures often follow victories.*

Before this event happened, David had just experienced a great victory in the area of demonstrating patience and love toward his enemy. King Saul had persistently tried to kill him. David could have snuffed out his life with a single thrust of his spear in a secluded cave where Saul lay sleeping. Why not even the score?

In his heart, David knew he could not—and would not! He loved his enemy who had again and again returned evil for good.

Nabal's insulting comments were minor compared to what Saul had attempted to do to David. Anyone who would stop to think for a moment would expect this kind of behavior from a fool. Nevertheless, David lost control of himself and almost committed mass murder.

As a Christian man, have you ever passed a big test in your life and then failed a little one? We all have—and we must be on guard at all times. We are most vulnerable when we are coming off our most successful experiences. This is why Paul warned us, "Let him who thinks he stands take heed lest he fall" (1 Cor. 10:12).

### *Principle 2. A wounded ego is a dangerous motivator.*

David's uncontrolled anger responded more to an attack on his self-image and ego than on his life. Saul tried to kill David many times—to wipe him off the face of the earth. By contrast, Nabal simply rejected him personally. With biting sarcasm, he denied he even knew who David was. This, of course, was a low blow to any man but hardly worth giving the time of day—let alone becoming angry enough to take the lives of innocent people lives.

All of us are most vulnerable to anger when we are personally attacked or put down. Sometimes it seems we can handle physical threats better than psychological threats. Let someone puncture our ego, attack our self-image, or tear down our public reputation, and we're in danger of losing control of our emotions—and our behavior. This is exactly what happened to David. This is why James wrote, "But let everyone be quick to hear, slow to speak and slow to anger" (James 1:19).

### *Principle 3. Decisions made in anger can be disastrous.*

Anyone in David's position would no doubt have experienced angry feelings. We're all human and we don't like to be rejected or humiliated. This kind of put-down is difficult to handle emotionally. David's mistake, however, was to make a decision and act on it while he was in a state of anger.

We all have this tendency. Being a Christian man does not exempt us from this kind of overreaction. This is why Paul warned us, "In your anger do not sin: Do not let the sun go down while you are still angry, and do not give the devil a foothold" (Eph. 4:26–27, NIV).

With this warning, Paul also acknowledged that not all anger is sin. Anger is a human emotion. It becomes sin, however, when we act in improper ways. This was David's mistake and if not for the grace of God—and the wisdom of Abigail—he would have committed a serious crime, one he would have regretted the rest of his life.

### *Principle 4. Quick-tempered responses are dangerous.*

A quick temper is a mark of immaturity in the life of any Christian man. This is why Paul warned both Timothy and Titus not to appoint men to leadership in the church who have this problem (1 Tim. 3:1–10; Titus 1:7).

David failed the test at this point in his life. If we're honest, we would all admit that we have faced this problem as well. Our goal should be to control our tempers, and when we lose them inappropriately, to correct the situation by asking forgiveness and making amends when we've hurt someone.

### *Principle 5. It's God's prerogative to take revenge.*

Because David's pride was hurt, he was determined to retaliate. Sadly, he even allowed his anger to focus on innocent people. Though one man was the source of his hurt and his anger, David was going to wipe out all of Nabal's manservants.

Abigail intervened—and David was eternally grateful. By his own confession, he had sought revenge—and he knew it would have been a terrible sin.

In this situation, God brought immediate judgment upon Nabal. We cannot, of course, expect God to respond this way in every situation. However, there will come a day when the Lord will settle all accounts of wrongdoing. Consequently, we must not return evil for evil. If we cannot settle such problems through mature dialogue and communication, we must leave them to God. It is His prerogative to settle these matters—and He will! (Rom. 12:17–21)

## Becoming a Man after God's Heart

Following are some suggestions for handling anger in yourself and others. Put a plus mark (+) by those suggestions where you feel you are doing well. Put a minus (-) where you feel you need improvement. Once you complete this exercise, select the area or areas where you need to focus in order to become a man after God's heart. Then set a goal. For example, you may tend to "counter anger with anger" rather than attempting to respond in a biblical fashion.

### *How to Handle Anger in Yourself*

1. Try not to be caught off-guard. We are often the most vulnerable when we feel we've got it all together.

2. Remember that anger often relates significantly to our self-image—and particularly a wounded ego. It's often easier to handle physical threats than psychological threats. Insecurity breeds quick tempers.

3. Don't make significant decisions and take specific actions when you're angry. Wait until you have regained control. It's often helpful to talk the problem out with a third person who will listen objectively and not get caught up in your emotions.

4. Deal with a quick temper. "Reprogram" your mind not to respond with threats and insecure reactions. Try to perceive every difficult situation as a learning experience rather than a personal attack.

5. Never try to get even or to take vengeance on someone who has hurt you. This does not mean you shouldn't communicate directly in attempting to straighten out a matter, but try to do so honestly, openly, and in a state of emotional control—and with the other person's interest at heart.

### *How to Handle Anger in Others*

1. Do not counter anger with anger. Remember that "A gentle answer turns away wrath, but a harsh word stirs up anger" (Prov. 15:1).

2. Attempt to understand the source of the anger. Realize that most people lose control because of a threat or because of events that have created frustration and anxiety. You may be witnessing "the straw that broke the camel's back." Try to put the person at ease, accepting his feelings. Remember the Proverb, "Pleasant words are a honeycomb, sweet to the soul and healing to the bones" (16:24).

3. Listen to the person carefully before responding. Try to get a perspective on the person's feelings—even if they are directed at you. Try not to take what is said personally.

4. Remember that people who are angry sometimes use others as scapegoats. Even though you may be the object of the attack, you may not be the primary source of frustration. Remember also this Proverb: "Like apples of gold in settings of silver is a word spoken in right circumstances" (25:11).

### *Set a Goal*

With God's help, I will begin immediately to carry out the following goal in my life:

______________________________________

______________________________________

______________________________________

______________________________________

______________________________________

### *Memorize the Following Scripture*

*This you know, my beloved brethren. But let everyone be quick to hear, slow to speak and slow to anger; for the anger of man does not achieve the righteousness of God.*

JAMES 1:19–20

Chapter 11

# *That Culprit Called Self-Deception*

Read 1 Samuel 27:1–28:2; 29:1–4; 30:1–20

*H*ave you ever faced a conflict so serious and painful that you made decisions which eventually left you in a worse state than before? Your initial decision seemed so logical—so rational! It seemed the only thing to do.

At first, things went a lot better. You felt great. You had more prestige. You made more money. You made more friends. Some of your enemies even seemed to be at peace with you. After all, you thought to yourself, how could God be displeased with my new lifestyle since I have all these benefits and blessings?

Sadly, you now understand you were rationalizing all along. You deceived yourself. It's now inconceivable that you could have made such foolish decisions. But you did! You now see that your thinking refocused only because you had nowhere to turn but back to God.

Thank God you turned back to Him! Isn't it wonderful that in His love and grace, God welcomed you back home, back to where you belong, and back into His perfect will?

## *David's Experience*

No one would deny that David faced incredible obstacles. Again and again he was threatened and rejected by the king of

Israel. He was betrayed by those who were supposed to be his friends. He and his little band of men were forced to travel hither and yon, looking for a place to hide from their enemies. When he experienced two unusual opportunities to take Saul's life—and was encouraged to do so by his own men—he "turned the other cheek" and spared the king of Israel.

## Rejection Is a Horrible Feeling

From our vantage point, we can see clearly that God was not rejecting David—or forsaking him. However, in the midst of his wilderness wanderings, David lost sight of God's protective hand. He began to experience deep feelings of isolation and rejection—not only from King Saul but from God.

Several of David's psalms reflect these feelings:

- "Why dost Thou stand afar off, O LORD? Why dost Thou hide Thyself in times of trouble?" (10:1)
- "How long, O LORD? Wilt Thou forget me forever? How long wilt Thou hide Thy face from me? How long shall I take counsel in my soul, having sorrow in my heart all the day? How long will my enemy be exalted over me?" (13:1–2)

David stated his deepest expression of grief and anxiety when he wrote:

- *"My God, my God, why hast Thou forsaken me?"* (22:1)

## Beware of Self-Pity

When we face what we believe are insurmountable problems, we often begin to feel sorry for ourselves. This is what happened to David. He was obsessed with self-pity and lost his perspective.

David's self-pity was rooted in logic. After all, he had turned the other cheek. He had gone the extra mile. He had just spared his archenemy, the king of Israel. Had he not been loyal and faithful both to his king on earth and to his King in heaven? Why weren't things going better?

Who would blame David for asking these questions? Self-pity took control and caused David to make decisions that were woefully out of God's will. Since God seemed to be absent, he decided he'd take matters into his own hands and solve the problems himself.

## Beware of Prayerlessness

David made his biggest mistake when he didn't consult God. Sound familiar? He made a key decision on his own. Listen to his thoughts: "Now I will perish one day by the hand of Saul. There is nothing better for me than to escape into the land of the Philistines. Saul then will despair of searching for me any more in all the territory of Israel, and I will escape from his hand" (1 Sam. 27:1).

David's "rationality" actually turned to "irrationality." To conclude that Saul eventually was going to kill him directly contradicted what God had promised.

God had clearly revealed through Samuel the prophet that David would be the next king of Israel (16:1). But, as often happens when we are absorbed with self-pity, we either forget God's Word or we lose faith in what God has said. This happened to David.

To conclude that there would be "nothing better" for him than "to escape into the land of the Philistines" was definitely in opposition to the will of God.

How many times had the Lord warned Israel never to develop relationships with pagan people? David, of all people, knew why God issued this command. The Lord didn't want His children to become like their pagan counterparts. He didn't want them to be influenced by pagan values. He constantly warned against worshiping their false gods.

You may be asking: Didn't David know in his heart he was violating God's command and subjecting his family and hundreds of other families to a pagan and degenerate environment?

Frankly, I don't think so. He was thinking first and foremost of himself—his anxieties, his problems, his fears and feelings of rejection. That's why he thought to himself, "There is nothing better for *ME* than to escape into the land of the Philistines." In the midst of his emotional misery, selfishness mastered his thoughts and he failed to think about others—including his own family and close friends.

## *"See, Everything's Going Great!"*

David fell prey to one of Satan's most subtle tricks. Once he made the decision to live among the Philistines, everything seemed to go better. He must have thought to himself, "Surely God's hand is in all of this!"

The pressure was off. Saul no longer tried to kill David. When the king discovered that "David had fled to Gath . . . he no longer searched for him" (27:4). For the first time in months—even years—David was free from the pressures of Saul's pursuit. It felt so good!

David also found acceptance at Gath, something he didn't have in the land of Israel. Even the king of Gath welcomed him. Ironically, this was the same king who had rejected him before when he feigned insanity (21:10,15). David must have thought to himself, "This is a miracle!"

Think of the fantastic tale David must have told Achish. Perhaps it went something like this:

> "King Achish, I spent many years serving Saul. I was his faithful armor-bearer. I won many of his battles. I even slew your giant Goliath—you remember that, sir. I was just a young boy. But Saul has never appreciated my loyalty. In fact, as you know, he has tried to take my life many times.
>
> "I have never been disloyal to King Saul, sir. I even had two recent opportunities to kill him. One was in a cave. He was asleep. I could have killed him with one blow. But I didn't. I spared his life. I consider him the Lord's anointed.

"Another opportunity came one night when Saul was sound asleep in the center of his camp. He was looking for me, trying to kill me. I slipped into the midst of the camp and stood beside him. There he was sound asleep. Again one blow would have killed him. But I didn't, Sir. I only took his spear and water bottle and left. Later I called to him trying to demonstrate that I was loyal. Though Saul confessed his own hatred toward me and promised me he would not hurt me, I could never trust him again. And sure enough, I was right. I've only experienced repeated rejection from him. If it please you, sir, provide me with a place of safety and I'll serve you rather than Saul. You can trust me."

## What More Could a King Want?

David must have related these facts to Achish. Furthermore, the king must have been impressed. After all, David's story definitely would have appealed to this man's ego. How ironic—and fortunate—to have at his disposal Saul's faithful servant-turned-traitor. What more could a king want than a way to discover the secrets of Israel's victories over the Philistines?

Achish was no fool. He knew that Israel's God had been with David. He knew David overcame Goliath "in the name of the LORD of hosts" (17:45a). Achish probably concluded that helping David would also give him an inside track to the "God of the armies of Israel" (v. 45b). After all, it seemed that "this God" guaranteed victories. Remember, too, that a pagan king who worshiped many gods would embrace another "god" in order to achieve his goals. The more gods, the better! To Achish, there was safety in "supernatural" numbers.

## From Better to Better

David's "smooth words" must have been very convincing. Why would an enemy of Israel trust David so much that he would actually give him and his followers a place of refuge? Perhaps it's because both of these men had one thing in common: an enemy named Saul. Achish certainly knew all about

Saul's repeated attempts on David's life. This helped David establish credibility with the Philistine king.

This was Satan's most insidious achievement. David and his band of followers were given a secure place to live—first in the royal city and eventually in their own city.

All of this developed one step at a time. At just the right moment, David approached the king once again and asked for another favor: "If now I have found favor in your sight, let them give me a place in one of the cities in the country, that I may live there; for why should your servant live in the royal city with you?" (27:5)

David was a super salesman. He appealed to his own unworthiness to live in the same city with King Achish. It worked! The king's answer was astonishing: "So Achish gave him Ziklag that day," an abandoned city which served as an ideal place for David's men and their families (v. 6). It was a city formerly inhabited by Israel and later captured by the Philistines.

If God were orchestrating all of this, we could understand why it was taking place. But David was walking straight out of the will of God. The Lord in no way could condone his behavior—or help him to achieve goals that were in opposition to His perfect will. This simply indicates how much we can accomplish with our own wisdom—and then rationalize as proof God is on our side.

## Saul's Men Desert Their King

In 1 Chronicles we discover that when the valiant warriors in Saul's army heard how Achish had accepted David and given him the city of Ziklag as a gift, many of these men deserted Saul and joined David. "For day by day men came to David to help him, until there was a great army like the army of God" (1 Chron. 12:22).

David's faithful six hundred soon turned into thousands. You can imagine how this bolstered David's self-image and reassured him that he had indeed made the right decision.

How easy it must have been for him to rationalize that this was all in God's plan to make him the next king.

## *David's Serious Problems Begin*

As always when we walk out of the will of God, trouble lies ahead. It may come suddenly or gradually, but eventually it will come—and it often multiplies rapidly. How true this was in David's life!

### Mouths to Feed

Predictably, one of David's first major problems was to provide food for his growing company of followers. Again David must have rationalized. He and his men invaded the Geshurites, the Gerzites and the Amalekites—most of whom were herdsmen (1 Sam. 27:8). Though these people were enemies of Israel, they had not provoked this battle. Furthermore, God gave no specific orders to make this attack, as He had in years gone by. Neither did the Lord give David permission to take any of their herds, flocks, or clothing (v. 9). This was simply a cruel and selfish maneuver orchestrated by David. The "end justified the means."

Since the people David attacked were friendly with the Philistines, what would Achish say when he heard? At this juncture, David had two alternatives. He could acknowledge what he had done and seek forgiveness from the king. Or he could keep Achish from finding out what happened.

Sadly, he chose the second alternative. In order to keep Achish from hearing about these atrocities, David slaughtered every person in the areas he attacked, including women and children—an act that later would haunt him (vv. 9,11). But at that moment, his rationale was that "dead men tell no tales."

### What About the Bounty?

David was getting in deeper. He could destroy the evidence of *who* he attacked, but he couldn't hide the fact that he had raided a group of people. The very reason he attacked these people became the reason Achish found out what happened. David could not hide the sheep, the cattle, the donkeys, the camels, and the clothing (vv. 9–10).

Sure enough, Achish asked, "Where have you made a raid today?" (v. 10) Again David had a choice. He could confess what he had done—or falsify the truth. David chose to tell a boldfaced lie!

Lies, however, are complicated. What would David say? What would make sense? David reported that he had attacked Israel—his own people. Since there was no evidence who these people really were, and since David's army was returning from the same direction as the border with Israel, David made his story convincing. "Achish believed David, saying, 'He has surely made himself odious among his people Israel; therefore he will become my servant forever'" (v. 12).

On the surface, David was gaining prestige in the eyes of the Philistine king. But in the eyes of God, he was sinking deeper and deeper into the mire of sin and walking farther and farther out of His will.

## Sin Exacts a Terrible Price!

For a time, David seemingly sidestepped the traps he had created for himself. Eventually, however, he wasn't wise enough to come up with the solution for every problem. His first real dilemma came when Achish decided to make war against Israel. This was something David had not anticipated. And, he had done such a great job establishing his credibility with King Achish that the king wanted David to go into battle with him (28:1). What was David to do? He had no excuse. He could only nod affirmatively. Imagine David's surprise when Achish told him he wanted to make him his personal bodyguard (v. 2).

For David to tell the truth would mean suicide—not only for himself but for all of his people. Furthermore, he was so indebted to this man of the world that it was impossible to back out. His only choice was to feign excitement about the prospect of going into battle against Israel—and to hope he could somehow get out of the mess he'd created. His scheme was coming unraveled!

## Amazing Grace

God's grace *is* amazing. When the Lord makes a promise, He keeps it. In spite of David's sin, God began to provide a way out of the quagmire he'd created.

The source of that grace was unexpected. Achish's military leaders were suspicious. They sensed their leader was deluded. They insisted David and his army not be allowed to join them in their fight against Israel lest he seize the opportunity to make an inside attack on the Philistines. What better way, they reasoned, could David gain merit in Saul's eyes (29:4)?

David was still trying to control his own destiny. He probably was so entangled in his web of sin that he didn't even recognize God's grace. Consequently he acted surprised and disappointed that he couldn't continue to prepare for the battle against Israel. Inwardly, however, he was breathing a sigh of relief. David had become a master prevaricator.

## The Roof Caves In

But David was about to reap the results of his sin. When his men returned to Ziklag, the city had been attacked by the Amalekites. They had burned it to the ground and taken captive all the women, children, and those men who had not joined David. Neither David nor his men knew whether their loved ones were dead or alive. David had to be thinking about his own merciless raid on the Amalekites. As a wise person once said, "What goes around comes around!"

In the midst of this horrible situation, everyone was terribly dejected. Sorrow and remorse burrowed deeply into their souls. They "lifted their voices and wept until there was no strength in them to weep" (30:4). But their sorrow soon turned to anger—so much so they wanted to stone David (v. 6).

At this moment, David reached a low point in his life. Suddenly what he had done over the last several months flashed before his eyes. Seeing himself as God saw him, he reached up once again to the Lord for help—perhaps for the first time since he had left Israel. We read that "David strengthened himself in the Lord his God" (v. 6). This was the beginning of his restoration.

## Seeking God's Will

David's actions reflect the man he once was—a man after God's own heart. The Lord gave him permission to pursue the Amalekites and when he did, he rescued every kidnapped loved one alive—another marvelous manifestation of God's grace in David's life (v. 19). God restored him and he once again began walking with the Lord.

## Becoming God's Man Today

*Principles to Live By*

David learned some painful lessons through this experience in the land of the Philistines. As Christian men (and women), we can learn some valuable lessons from his life and avoid the circumstances and decisions that caused such desperate pain. This is why God is so explicit in the Old Testament in outlining the sins of even his most respected servants. He wants us to learn from their failures (1 Cor. 10:11).

### *Principle 1. We must beware of the effects of self-pity.*

We all feel sorry for ourselves at certain times in our lives, but we must be doubly cautious when self-pity grows out of a sense of rejection. It can very easily lead to very self-centered decisions that eventually lead in turn to disaster.

This was David's problem. He felt rejected both by Saul and by God. Consequently he made his decisions based on his own personal needs, without regard for others or God's will. Needless to say, it led to serious consequences.

*Principle 2. We must beware of losing perspective on God's plan for our lives.*

There will be periods of confusion and darkness in our lives. But we must attempt to think long-range. Some of these periods come because God is testing us. Others come simply because we are living in a sinful world. But in all of these circumstances, God wants us to wait out the storm. He wants us to know that His "grace is sufficient" and His "power is perfected in weakness" (2 Cor. 12:9).

David lost perspective on God's will for his life. In the midst of this wilderness experience, he forgot the promises of God and was unable even to remember God's previous protection and care.

*Principle 3. We must not interpret blessings in our lives as necessarily a sign that God has always approved of our decisions.*

Some Christians make this mistake and justify making decisions that contradict God's revealed will. I've heard people say, "But I feel so much better separated from my wife or husband." Or, "God must be pleased with what I'm doing; otherwise, why would I be making so much money?"

Obviously, an unhappy relationship in marriage yields to emotional relief when the stress is eliminated. The same dynamic held true in David's life. He felt better when he was out from under Saul's persecution. But this did not mean he was walking in the will of God.

Regarding material blessings, remember that God "causes His sun to rise on the evil and the good, and sends rain on the righteous and the unrighteous" (Matt. 5:45). David's mistake was that he interpreted the blessings and acceptance he received in the land of the Philistines as a sign of God's approval.

*Principle 4. We must never take advantage of God's grace.*

God *does* love us. We are His children. He'll never reject us or disown us. His love is infinite. Nothing "shall be able to separate us from the love of God, which is in Christ Jesus our Lord" (Rom. 8:39).

But God *will* discipline us (Heb. 12:7–11). In many instances, this discipline consists of allowing us to suffer the natural consequences of our sin—which may not be obvious immediately. But the problems *will come*—just as they did in David's life. In the process, we not only will hurt ourselves but we also will hurt those closest to us. Furthermore, we may hurt other innocent people. Think of those women and children David massacred!

If we understand God's grace, we'll never take advantage of this wonderful gift. Rather, we'll be taught by it. This is why Paul wrote to Titus:

> The grace of God that brings salvation has appeared to all men. It teaches us to say "No" to ungodliness and worldly passions, and to live self-controlled, upright and godly lives in this present age, while we wait for the blessed hope—the glorious appearing of our great God and Savior, Jesus Christ, who gave himself for us to redeem us from all wickedness and to purify for himself a people that are his very own, eager to do what is good. (Titus 2:11–14, NIV)

### *Principle 5. We must never conclude that it's too late to turn back to God.*

Though we may have to reap what we have sown, God's grace and forgiveness are always available to all who call upon Him, whether Christian or non-Christian. When David reached his lowest point, when he had nowhere to turn, when his own self-centered strategies ultimately failed—he "strengthened himself in the Lord his God." He acknowledged his sin. He once again began to walk in God's ways.

We must never let pride stand in our way. Remember that "everyone who calls on the name of the Lord will be saved" (Rom. 10:13 NIV). Furthermore, "If we confess our sins, he is faithful and just and will forgive us our sins and purify us from all unrighteousness" (1 John 1:9 NIV). We must remember that there's no sin too great for God to forgive and forget!

## Becoming a Man after God's Heart

Use the following lessons from David's life as checkpoints in your own life. Which ones apply to you? Isolate your own area of need and decide today that you are going to refocus your life in that particular area. Then set a goal. For example, you may tend to take advantage of God's grace in the way you live as a Christian.

*Personal Checkpoints*

____ 1. I am prone to self-pity and selfish decisions that lead me out of the will of God.

____ 2. I easily lose perspective on God's plan for my life, which also leads to improper decisions.

____ 3. I sometimes interpret blessings in my life as a sign of God's approval on my disobedience.

____ 4. I tend to take advantage of God's grace in the way I live as a Christian.

____ 5. I am at a low point in my life and I need to turn back to God.

*Set a Goal*

With God's help, I will begin immediately to carry out the following goal in my life:

____________________________________________

____________________________________________

____________________________________________

____________________________________________

____________________________________________

## *Memorize the Following Scripture*

> *For the grace of God has appeared, bringing salvation to all men, instructing us to deny ungodliness and worldly desires and to live sensibly, righteously and godly in the present age.*
>
> TITUS 2:11–12

Chapter 12

# *David's Tragic Moral Failure*

Read 2 Samuel 11:1–12:23

*I* once knew a pastor I often think of as "a man after God's heart!" Our close relationship spanned more than twenty years of mutual ministry. But, like David, he became sexually involved with a woman who was not his wife. The results—as always—were tragic!

Thankfully, this man has worked hard to rebuild his marriage, his family, and his reputation. That's one reason I still believe he is "a man after God's heart!" However, long after he was caught in this sin, had confessed it openly and sought forgiveness, he continued to be deceitful and manipulative. It took months for him to accept full responsibility for his actions and to stop rationalizing.

## *A Tangled Web*

During this difficult period, he hurt many people—probably more than he has ever realized. But, he did not sink to the same level as David and "take another man's life as well as his wife." However, during the period he was involved in this affair, he worked overtime trying to resolve the problem he had created. But the damage was done! He was trapped in his sin. Try as he might he could not disentangle himself. Like so many men who get involved in this kind of relationship, he lived a double life.

## The Proverbial Smoke Screen

In order to cover his own sin, this man used a technique as old as history itself. Adam first used it in the Garden of Eden when he told the Lord that the problem was the woman God had given him (Gen. 3:12). He tried to get the focus off of his problem and onto someone else—in this instance, his wife, Eve.

Though the method was different, the dynamics were the same with the man I am writing about. He kept trying to come up with a way "to leave the scene" without losing his pastoral position and his reputation.

He believed his best option was to start another church, using as his nucleus people who had grown to love him in his current ministry. To achieve his goal, he began giving the impression he could no longer work with the senior leader because of conflicts in the relationship. If people really believed he needed to start this new church because he couldn't work with his fellow pastor, he'd have a logical reason to leave as well as a base of support. Somehow, he felt he could "cover his sin" and continue as if nothing had happened.

Irrational? Yes, but that's exactly what David did. He was so self-deceived that he thought he could cover his sin by removing Uriah, Bathsheba's husband. In a sense, this is what my friend was trying to do to his fellow pastor. If only he could get this man on the "front lines" and somehow "get the focus off of himself," then perhaps he could escape without being discovered.

## Blind-Sided by a Friend

All during this period, the senior pastor didn't know what was happening. He sensed something was wrong in the relationship—but he had no idea what this man was doing behind the scenes. For one thing, they had been long-time friends. In fact, this man trapped in sin had publicly defended his fellow pastor when others had accused him falsely in the past. In situations like this, it's difficult even to contemplate such a betrayal. However, once the sin was discovered, everything made sense. The fog cleared!

You may wonder how such a "good man" could get trapped in this kind of sinful pattern of behavior. But think for a moment; This is exactly what happened to David, and he was a good man—a man after God's heart! I also know from this experience that it can happen to *any* man who allows himself to indulge in sexual sin.

## *Saul's Suicide*

Following David's repentance and restoration for seeking refuge in the land of the Philistines, the next major event that affected his life dramatically was Saul's death on the battlefield on Mount Gilboa. Sadly, Saul took his own life (1 Sam. 31:3–5).

How thankful David must have been that God had delivered him from having to join the Philistine army to do battle against Israel—the very battle in which Saul and David's soul brother, Jonathan, lost their lives. Had he been party to the death of the Lord's anointed and his best friend, he never would have forgiven himself. As it was, his mourning for them reflected deep sorrow and love, which revealed the David whose heart could be so right toward God and man (2 Sam. 1).

## *Days of Transition*

Following Saul's death, the events leading to David's kingship gradually unfolded. He served as king of Judah for seven and one-half years, and then was crowned as ruler of all Israel.

These days of transition were generally good for David. He walked with God and consulted Him. He demonstrated great wisdom and justice in Israel. He waited for God's timing in the matters before him. He experienced numerous victories over the enemies of Israel and eventually established Jerusalem as a capital city. David "stood tall" as one of the greatest spiritual leaders in Old Testament history.

Nearly twenty years after David first occupied the throne, however, he committed one of the greatest sins of his life. Though it eventually was forgiven, David's moral failure continued to pay its wages for many years in his life, in the lives of his family, and in all Israel.[1]

## *How It Happened*

David had been actively involved in leading the armies of Israel against their enemies. Through his leadership, they had defeated nearly everyone who was a threat to their national security. At this point in his life, David was relatively free from military responsibility. He gladly turned over his military role to Joab, his faithful commander, who could easily handle any skirmishes against the enemies of Israel.

No one would deny that David had earned the right to relax and enjoy his position as king. He was now about fifty years old, having spent many of those years in active duty as a warrior on the front lines. He had paid his dues!

### A Leisurely Afternoon

One afternoon while David was lying down to rest, he couldn't sleep. He arose from his bed and went out on the roof of his house—a vantage point that gave him a bird's-eye view of most of Jerusalem. As he walked about viewing the city, perhaps contemplating his success as king, he couldn't help noticing a woman who was bathing on a nearby rooftop. The Bible states that she was "*very* beautiful in appearance" (2 Sam. 11:2). David quickly responded to what he saw. He found out who she was, sent for her and committed adultery.

### Was David Seduced?

Some Bible scholars believe Bathsheba may have been trying to seduce David. This, of course, is feasible since she no doubt had noticed the king on many occasions strolling on his rooftop. Perhaps she was purposely trying to attract his attention.

But even if this be true, what David did is inexcusable. He had openly violated God's law and taken another man's wife (Exod. 20:14,17). He was responsible for his own actions!

## "Be Sure Your Sins Will Find You Out!"

In David's mind the event was over. But Bathsheba conceived.

Had David been just another of the pagan kings who ruled at that time, he could have solved the problem quickly and easily. He simply could have taken Bathsheba into his own household—not caring what happened to her husband. Or he could have ignored her plight. Since a king was considered sovereign by his people, he could do anything he wanted. He was above the law; he made the laws. In most of the neighboring kingdoms, no lawgiver was superior to the kings themselves.

## No Ordinary King

But David had been "anointed by God." He served a Lawgiver far superior to himself—One who had thundered from Mount Sinai many years before: "You shall not commit adultery. . . . You shall not covet your neighbor's house; you shall not covet your neighbor's wife or his male servant or his female servant or his ox or his donkey or anything that belongs to your neighbor" (Exod. 20:14,17).

David had sinned against his own King. It was his greatest failure! Worse, he regressed to his old pattern of behavior and refused to acknowledge his sin. In fact, he may have talked himself into believing he was above God's law as king. However, he knew he was facing a serious crisis and he attempted to solve the problem all by himself. But as always happens in situations like this, he only got more entangled in his web of wrongdoing.

## David's Initial Scheme

David's first attempt to extricate himself from this predicament with the most logical idea he could think of: "I'll send for

Uriah, Bathsheba's husband," he thought. "I'll make him believe that I've sent for him to find out the welfare of Joab and the state of war. Then I'll give him some time off to spend with his wife. He'll never know the child is mine" (see 2 Sam. 11:6–8).

Thus David reasoned and thus he acted! This sounds like the David we met in the land of the Philistines twenty years earlier. One sin led to another then—now he is giving a repeat performance. Circumstances were different, but the spiritual dynamics were the same. If we don't admit our sin, confess it and seek forgiveness, we'll try to cover it up. This was David's plan.

To David's surprise, his simple, logical scheme didn't work. His great wisdom that had defeated armies could not deliver him from this self-imposed predicament. Uriah would not go home—which should have brought humiliating shame to David's heart. In fact, Uriah "slept at the door of the king's house with all the servants of his lord" (v. 9). He was so loyal to David and his fellow soldiers who were camping in the open battlefield that he would not allow himself the indulgence of staying in the comforts of his own home, enjoying his wife's favors.

## David's Second Scheme

David next devised a plan to blur Uriah's thinking and dull his sensitive spirit. He purposely got Uriah drunk, hoping he would stumble on home and forget his military responsibilities—at least for one evening.

But again David's strategy failed. Even in his drunken stupor, Uriah would not go home. He stayed in the king's court and slept in the servants' quarters.

## David's Third Scheme

By this time David was terribly frustrated. What was he going to do? He was both scared and angry—two emotions that frequently go together in a guilty heart.

In his state of emotional turmoil, David made a decision that is incredible—especially in view of his personal relationship with God. He decided to have Uriah killed—"legitimately," that is—in battle. David would then be free, at least in the eyes of Israel, to take Bathsheba as one of his wives. No one except the cooperating parties would know.

David wrote a letter to his commanding officer, ironically sending it via Uriah himself. He instructed Joab to send Uriah to the front lines. When the battle was most intense, Joab was to withdraw protection from Uriah and allow him to go it alone.

What makes this scheme so diabolical is that David knew Uriah would not retreat. He was too loyal! He'd already proved that point when the first two schemes failed. David actually used Uriah's commitment to him as the king of Israel in order to take his life.

As the world knows, the scheme worked. Uriah fell in battle. When word came of his death, David then brought Bathsheba "to his house and she became his wife" (v. 27). As far as David was concerned, he was "home free."

Again, if David had been an ordinary pagan king, life *would* have gone on as usual. But, David was God's anointed! Consequently, we read that "the thing that David had done was evil in the sight of the LORD" (v. 27). Not only did he violate the law of God by committing adultery, but in his efforts to cover up his sin, he lied, stole what did not belong to him, and committed murder. All of these acts violated specific laws of God who had thundered from Sinai: "You shall not *steal.* You shall not bear *false witness against your neighbor.* . . . You shall not *murder*" (Exod. 20:15–16,13).

## *A Story David Never Forgot*

For nearly a year David was able to cover his sin—refusing to acknowledge it to himself, to the Lord, and to the people of Israel. Then one day a strange thing happened. The Lord sent

Nathan the prophet to see David. Nathan told the king a story he never forgot:

> There were two men in one city, the one rich and the other poor.
> The rich man had a great many flocks and herds.
> But the poor man had nothing except one little ewe lamb
> Which he bought and nourished;
> And it grew up together with him and his children.
> It would eat of his bread and drink of his cup and lie in his bosom,
> And was like a daughter to him.
> Now a traveler came to the rich man,
> And he was unwilling to take from his own flock or his own herd,
> To prepare for the wayfarer who had come to him;
> Rather he took the poor man's ewe lamb and prepared it for the man who had come to him.
> (2 Sam. 12:1–4)

As David listened to Nathan's story, he became very angry at the rich man who had taken the poor man's only lamb. His sense of justice rose within him and he interrupted Nathan's story with words of judgment: "As the LORD lives, surely the man who has done this deserves to die. And he must make restitution for the lamb fourfold, because he did this thing and had no compassion" (vv. 5–6).

## Psychological Projection

David was so self-deceived that he didn't understand that he was pronouncing judgment on himself. He was so blinded that he couldn't see "the king of Israel" in the story. But in his anger, he was projecting his own repressed guilt and anxiety.

The intensity of his projection is seen in his exaggerated reaction. The Law of Moses clearly stated that under these conditions a man only needed to give back four sheep for the one he had stolen (Exod. 22:1). David's response was that a man like this "deserves to die."

David was speaking about himself and didn't realize it. God, who knows the depths of men's hearts, turned Nathan into a master psychologist.

### "You Are the Man!"

Nathan moved from storytelling to interpretation—and confrontation! In the midst of David's emotional identification and reactions, he suddenly pulled David's mask from his blinded eyes so he could see his self-deception. "You are the man!" cried Nathan (2 Sam. 12:7).

Nathan's words plunged like a knife into David's heart! His anger turned to grief and remorse. His fiery verbal attack turned to meekness and shame. His world of greatness suddenly crumbled around him as he saw himself for what he was—an adulterer, a liar, a thief, and a murderer! *He* was the man who deserved to die. David himself had sentenced men to death for lesser crimes against the laws of God!

## *God's Immeasurable Mercy*

Though David clearly deserved the death penalty (Lev. 20:10; 24:17), God forgave him because of his repentant and remorseful heart. Even in the Old Testament, we see God's grace shine in His dealings with His children. David's experience with the Lord highlights that grace like no other Old Testament event.

### The Natural Consequences of Sin

But God did not eliminate the natural consequences of this sin. His judgment on David was twofold. First, the child who was born to Bathsheba died—which caused David terrible grief (2 Sam. 12:15–20). This was immediate; the second consequence was long-range. David's own household would suffer a constant state of upheaval for the rest of his life. It happened just as God said it would (vv. 10–12). One of David's sons, Amnon, raped his sister Tamar. Absalom, another of David's sons, became so angry at Amnon for his terrible deed against their sister that he murdered his brother (2 Sam. 13).

This was just the beginning of sorrows for David. In time, Absalom rebelled against him and turned the hearts of the children of Israel against his own father. David had to leave Jerusalem and flee for his life with just a few faithful followers.

Eventually Absalom attacked David in battle (chaps. 14–18). However, while attempting to murder his own father, Absalom lost his own life—adding sorrow upon sorrow to David's heart (18:15).

The sword never departed from David's household—just as God foretold (12:10). Even his wise son, Solomon, who eventually replaced David as the king of Israel, followed in his father's footsteps and disobeyed God in many of the same areas David did.

Yes, God forgave David and preserved his life. But what a horrible price to pay for a moment of pleasure!

## *Ten Points to Remember*

*1. David had experienced an unprecedented period of success both in his personal life and in his relationship with the children of Israel.* Though David faced the same routine problems we all face, he had lived a godly life relatively free from serious sin for nearly twenty years. He had brought security and safety to his people. This was also a high point in Israel's history and its witness to the outside world. The Israelites had demonstrated an unusual commitment to God and to each other. All of this was a reflection of David's excellent leadership.

It was following this period of success and his brilliant career as king of Israel—demonstrating wisdom, justice, and righteousness—that David committed the most unwise, unjust, and unrighteous act of his life.

*2. When the temptation came, David was idle, with little to do but relax and enjoy his position as king.* David had lived a very busy life. But at this moment, he had not had so much leisure time since his days as a shepherd boy. While he was busy "doing nothing" he became vulnerable to Satan's attack. Rather than filling his thoughts with God and His greatness as he had done in his younger years, David allowed his mind to think about himself and his needs. It was his idleness and boredom that became the Devil's workshop.

3. *As a king, David could do almost anything he wanted and get anything he desired.* David's central problem was not a cold, uncaring wife who didn't love him or meet his emotional and physical needs. If it had been, his behavior might have been more understandable—while still inexcusable. David had wives and concubines galore, many of whom were ready and willing to spend an evening with the king. Unmet sexual needs were not his problem!

David's primary problem was rooted in the fact that he knew he could do almost anything and get away with it. After all, he was a king! Hadn't he unselfishly given himself to help Israel find security and direction in its life as a nation? David may have rationalized that he had a "right" to spend an evening with Bathsheba.

I vividly remember spending several days with a well-known pastor who had committed adultery with various women. I'll never forget his confession. He acknowledged that he came to the place where he talked himself into believing he deserved these moments of pleasure because he "worked so hard for God" and built such a large church. He believed the trysts were "perks" for being so diligent.

This kind of rationalization comes easily to people in the habit of being successful. They want what they want—when they want it! Gradually many become a law unto themselves, throwing all moral values to the wind—even those they once defended. Apparently David fell into this trap.

4. *David had violated God's law in multiplying wives and concubines.* Even though God allowed polygamy in Old Testament

times, it was never His ideal plan. If it had been, He would have created more than one wife for Adam—or more than one husband for Eve. His perfect plan was that these two people find fellowship and fulfillment in each other.

However, when sin entered the world, it affected God's perfect plan, including the area of sexual relationships. Because sin became so pervasive in the world of the Old Testament, God tolerated polygamy, but He never willed it. Furthermore, we note that whenever it happened, there were always serious problems, such as jealousy, quarreling, crime, and sensual indulgence.

It's important to note that God specifically forbade what David did. In the law which he revealed to Moses, the Lord specifically warned that no future king of Israel should ever "multiply wives for himself, lest his heart turn away" (Deut. 17:17). David ignored this law, which set the stage for what happened with Bathsheba.

Neither can we overlook the element of pride in what David did. Pagan kings—being the only ones who normally could afford large harems—took great pride in their female-possessions. David fell prey to this worldly mentality in order to demonstrate his greatness as a king. The results were devastating.

*5. David allowed temptation to turn into an act of sin.* No one would fault David for responding emotionally to what he saw. Bathsheba was a beautiful woman. His initial temptation and desire were not acts of sin. His disobedience came when he lusted in his heart. He deliberately sought her out for the purpose of having a sexual relationship.

*6. David did not acknowledge his sin immediately and take action to correct it.* David's unwillingness to face his sin quickly led to more serious sins—including murder. This was not a new development. Twenty years before, he faced the same dilemma in the land of the Philistines. One sin led to another when he tried to work it out by himself. In that situation God delivered David from his own connivings before his actions became irreversible.

7. *David denied the reality of this sin and consequently deceived himself.* Apparently, the guilt and anxiety in David's heart became so great that he repressed his wrongdoing from his conscious thoughts. This is apparent in his reaction to Nathan's story. He saw no relationship between the facts Nathan related in this illustration and what he had done to Uriah.

8. *David took advantage of God's grace once too often, and suffered terrible consequences.* When David was about to kill innocent shepherds because of Nabal's personal rejection, God used Abigail to stop him. Had he done what he intended to do, it would have been a terrible blight on his reputation as the future king of Israel.

On another occasion, when David was about to enter a battle with the Philistine army against Israel, God again delivered him from a predicament he had created for himself.

David demonstrates that there comes a time in a man's life when he must bear the responsibility for his own actions. When the king of Israel decided to commit adultery with Bathsheba, God "stepped aside" and allowed him to engage in a horrible sin. He also didn't stop David from carrying out his diabolical plan to take the life of Uriah. David had taken advantage of God's grace one time too often.

9. *The consequences of David's sins were far greater than they would have been for the average man on the street.* David was the spiritual and political leader in Israel. All eyes were on him. He had been known most of his life as "a man after God's own heart." Consequently, the results of this sin were far-reaching. Those most affected were his own family members, but the results of David's sin extended to all Israel. He lost the respect of his own people and even the pagans of the land.

10. *Though David, many of his loved ones, and all of Israel suffered the consequences of his sin, God forgave David because of*

*his sincere confession and contrite heart.* David's prayer for forgiveness is recorded in Psalm 51. Again, we see "a man after God's heart"—in spite of his terrible sin. Read these words carefully and prayerfully:

*David's Contrite Prayer*

Be gracious to me, O God, according to Thy
lovingkindness;
According to the greatness of Thy compassion blot out my
transgressions.
Wash me thoroughly from my iniquity,
And cleanse me from my sin.
For I know my transgressions,
And my sin is ever before me.
Against Thee, Thee only, I have sinned,
And done what is evil in Thy sight,
So that Thou art justified when Thou dost speak,
And blameless when Thou dost judge.

Purify me with hyssop, and I shall be clean;
Wash me; and I shall be whiter than snow.
Make me to hear joy and gladness,
Let the bones which Thou hast broken rejoice.
Hide Thy face from my sins,
And blot out all my iniquities.
Create in me a clean heart, O God,
And renew a steadfast spirit within me.
(Psalm 51:1–4; 7–10)

God answered David's prayer. He was once again at peace with His Heavenly Father. We see the results of that restored relationship in Psalm 32:

*God's Merciful Answer*

How blessed is the man to whom the LORD does not
impute iniquity,

And in whose spirit there is no deceit!
When I kept silent about my sin, my body wasted away
Through my groaning all day long.
For day and night Thy hand was heavy upon me;
My vitality was drained away as with the fever
heat of summer.
I acknowledged my sin to Thee,
And my iniquity I did not hide;
I said, "I will confess my transgressions to the LORD";
And Thou didst forgive the guilt of my sin."
(Psalm 32:2–5)

## Becoming God's Man Today

*Principles to Live By*

What we've just observed regarding David's sin translates into some very powerful principles for every man.

### *Principle 1. Never rely on past success as security from future failure.*

At any moment, at any hour, any Christian anywhere can be caught off-guard and fail God miserably. Most of our failures may not be as serious as David's. But they can be!

This principle particularly applies to Christian leaders. Moral failure is often the culprit, and this problem seems to be gaining momentum. Satan is having a heyday.

When it happens, the results devastate individual families and local churches—and the Body of Christ at large. This kind of failure also becomes a tragic stumbling block to non-Christians. The story of David has written across it in "flashing red lights" the words of Paul: "If you think you are standing firm, be careful that you don't fall!" (1 Cor. 10:12, NIV)

### *Principle 2. Avoid idleness and boredom.*

This doesn't mean Christians can't enjoy having periods of relaxation and vacations. We all need to rest and recuperate.

But even then, we must be on guard. Many a Christian man has fallen prey to Satan when he has been "busy doing nothing."

### *Principle 3. Remember that successful men often are very vulnerable to rationalization in their sexual lives.*

It's easy to want what we want when we want it. If we're not careful, we'll become a law unto ourselves and throw all moral values to the wind—even those we have most defended.

### *Principle 4. Be on guard against developing a sensuous lifestyle.*

Men in our culture may not be "polygamists" in the strict sense of that word, but many men are having multiple sexual experiences with a variety of people. This happens particularly to men who have not come to Christ personally. We are particularly vulnerable to Satan's attacks in this area of our lives—even after we become Christians. If you are a Christian coming out of this kind of background, beware! Satan is standing ready to trip you up at the slightest provocation.

### *Principle 5. Don't allow temptation to turn into sin.*

Temptation per se is not sin. However, any desire that we might have is only one step away from the act. Remember also that Jesus said an *intent to sin* is as wrong as the act itself. This is what our Lord meant when He said, "But I tell you that anyone who looks at a woman lustfully [a plan to commit sin] has already committed adultery with her in his heart" (Matt. 5:28, NIV).

### *Principle 6. Never cover up or hide sin.*

This is our first temptation once we fail. It's particularly difficult to admit sin when we know it will lead to embarrassment. However, if we cover our sin, we will not prosper. Furthermore, we are vulnerable to continuing the sin. And as we've seen in David's life, the more he tried to hide the first sin, the more he committed additional sins. Avoid this predicament by facing the sin immediately and confessing it to God. When necessary, confess it to others you have sinned against. Also, confess it to a trusted friend—another man—who can hold you accountable.

### *Principle 7. Acknowledge sin immediately—especially to God.*

The best way to handle guilt and anxiety is through confession. We must not repress these feelings. If we do, it will eventually lead to self-deception, a hardened heart, and a seared conscience.

### *Principle 8. Don't take advantage of God's grace.*

Remember, the Bible says there comes a time when "God gives man up" to do what he wants to do. Though this is spoken specifically to people who have turned away from God completely, I believe the principle still applies to Christians. When this happens, it is part of God's discipline in our lives. To reap what we sow is sometimes the most painful kind of consequence.

### *Principle 9. Remember that the greater our responsibility, the greater our accountability.*

The higher our position in the Christian world, the greater our potential fall. The more people who are involved in our lives, the more will be hurt through our failures.

### *Principle 10. No matter what the sin and its consequences, confess it and do what is right.*

The Bible teaches that the blood of Jesus Christ cleanses from all unrighteousness (1 John 1:9). No sin is too great to be forgiven. This is why we must accept God's forgiveness in Jesus Christ.

At this point, we must follow David's example. After he confessed his sin and received forgiveness, he accepted the consequences of his sin. Then he "arose from the ground, washed, anointed himself, and changed his clothes; and he came into the house of the Lord and worshiped" (2 Sam. 12:20).

## Becoming a Man after God's Heart

Evaluate your own lifestyle in the light of the lessons we've just learned from David's experience. As you review these principles, check any where you are particularly weak and vulnerable. Then set a goal. For example, your tendency may be to cover up or hide your sin.

*Check Yourself!*

____ Never rely on past success as security from future failure.

____ Avoid idleness and boredom.

____ Remember that successful men are often very vulnerable to rationalization in their sexual lives.

____ Be on guard against developing a sensual lifestyle.

____ Don't allow temptation to turn into sin.

____ Never cover up or hide sin.

____ Acknowledge sin immediately—especially to God.

____ Don't take advantage of God's grace.

____ Remember that the greater our responsibility, the greater our accountability.

____ No matter what the sin and its consequences, confess it and do what is right.

*Set a Goal*

With God's help, I will begin immediately to carry out the following goal in my life:

______________________________________________

______________________________________________

______________________________________________

______________________________________________

*Memorize the Following Scripture*

*Therefore, there is now no condemnation for those who are in Christ Jesus, because through Christ Jesus the law of the Spirit of life set me free from the law of sin and death.*

ROMANS 8:1–2, NIV

Chapter 13

# *David's Life in Perspective*

Read 1 Samuel 16:1–2 Samuel 24:25

Together we've looked at several major events in David's life. They yield dynamic principles that can help us live more victorious lives in our culture. However, so as not to miss some of the richest lessons from this Old Testament character, we need to look back over his life. It's not possible to observe these overarching principles unless we see the specifics unfold over a period of years and understand how these events relate to each other.

None of the experiences in our lives is an isolated event. They're all interrelated. This also holds true in David's life. We can see the ebb and flow in his experience, the ups and downs, the victories and the failures. Most importantly, this perspective will give us insights into why David did what he did on his journey through life.

### *Principle 1. God anointed David as king of Israel on the basis of his heart attitude at the time of his anointing.*

This truth is difficult to comprehend. God is omniscient and sovereign. He knows the end from the beginning and every detail in between. He controls the universe. His perspective is eternal.

Yet He instructed Samuel to anoint David on the basis of his spiritual condition as a young shepherd who loved and honored his heavenly Father. When Saul, of his own free will, *chose* to disobey God—he did so in the course of space and time. It was *then* that the Lord "sought out for Himself a man after His own heart" (1 Sam. 13:14).

David was that man. He chose him because of this young shepherd's view of God's attributes—His omnipotence, His omniscience, His omnipresence, His loving concern, His faithfulness, His righteousness, and His holiness. He selected David because of David's own heart, which was characterized by faith, thankfulness, honesty, openness, expectancy, humility, dependence, and repentance. Because of these qualities, God instructed Samuel to anoint David as the future king of Israel.

### *David's Failures Were Not Foreordained*

David's life story reveals he was not always the kind of person described above. There were periods when he ceased being a "man after God's own heart." He woefully failed God, did his own thing, walked directly and deliberately out of the will of God, and indulged in some incredible sins.

Because of His omniscience, the Lord knew David would fail Him in these areas of his life before He even chose him. But it was not within God's predetermined plan that David fail. In some remarkable way, the sovereign God of the universe anointed David to be king of Israel based upon his spiritual successes in the here and now, regardless of his future failures.

### *How Can This Be?*

There is no satisfactory human explanation. We can only cry out, "God, we don't understand," and then acknowledge that God is God and He can do it without violating His omniscience and His providence. The truth is that David could have been a "man after God's own heart" *all* of his life if he had always obeyed God and lived by the spiritual guidelines he followed as a young dedicated Hebrew.

The same opportunity lay before King Saul, who was anointed by God and promised continual blessing if he only walked in the Lord's ways (12:14). Like David's, Saul's failures were not predetermined. In fact, God was terribly distressed when Saul disobeyed Him. Twice we read that "the LORD regretted that He had made Saul king over Israel" (15:35; see also 15:11).

How can a sovereign God regret His own decisions when He knows the end from the beginning? Again, there is no satisfactory human explanation. It's beyond our finite minds. If we try to explain this concept totally, we end up with an extreme theological position that ignores certain realities in Scripture. In some remarkable and incomprehensible way, God honors man's freedom and makes His decisions accordingly. And, as shown in David's life, part of that decision-making process involves dealing with us at any given period in our lives.

### *What About You?*

God also deals with us on the basis of our *present* heart attitudes. The fact that we have warm, sensitive hearts toward God *now* is no guarantee that we will be that kind of person ten, twenty, or thirty years from now. God is using us *now* to achieve His purposes because of our present spiritual status and commitment to Him. However, this is no guarantee He will use us in the future. If we—like David—eventually ignore God's will, we too will have to pay the natural consequences.

### *A Sobering Story*

I've seen this very thing happen to one of my closest friends. He was a man who was sensitive toward God and people. He was one of the best Bible teachers I've ever known. He graduated from seminary with the highest honors, earning a doctorate in theology.

I saw many people's lives change because of this man's ministry. But little by little, he turned aside from obeying the Word of God. It was subtle and gradual. Today he is divorced from his wife and separated from his family. Hopefully, like David, he'll come to his senses one day and once again become a man after God's heart. If he does, God will forgive him and restore him—though he will have to face the natural consequences of his sin for the rest of his life.

David's example speaks to each of us. What we are *now*, and how God is using us *now* certainly is no guarantee for the future. It depends on our continual commitment to the Lord and our constant obedience.

### *Principle 2. David's failures always related to the fact that he failed to consult God regarding His will; conversely, his restoration always correlated with renewed communication with God.*

David was a man after God's heart because he spent many hours in personal communion with his heavenly Father. He had a great capacity for "hearing" and "seeing" God in what He created—upon the waters, in the wind, through the lightning and the thunder, in the rain showers, upon the green meadows and valleys, and as the golden grain was harvested (Pss. 29, 65).

David also was one of those Old Testament saints who experienced reciprocal communication with God. He often sought God's will about certain decisions and received a direct answer from the Lord. However, in each instance where he walked out of God's will, there is no evidence that he asked God about the matter. In fact, he even ignored the truths that God had already revealed.

It's also true that each time David refocused his spiritual life, he once again consulted the Lord. This was true following the tremendous bout with fear which led him to scheme and lie in order to escape from Saul (1 Sam. 21). Once he came to his senses, his first action was to seek God's will through prayer (23:4,10–12). The Lord in His love and grace answered him and gave him specific directions.

We see this same pattern when David lost complete perspective and sought asylum in the land of the Philistines. He didn't consult the Lord at all. He made his own decisions based upon his own human emotions and reactions. This time he managed to get into even deeper trouble.

But as before, he eventually regained perspective. When he did, one of his first responses was prayer. After what appears to be more than a year with no direct communication with the Lord, David once again "strengthened himself in the LORD his God" (30:6). Then he found himself back on the straight and narrow path, doing what God wanted him to do.

*What About You?*

Once again the lesson is clear! If we are to *remain* in God's will throughout our lifetime, we must seek God's will. We must consult the Lord.

*God's Voice Today*

Today God has not chosen as a normal means of communication to speak to His children by direct revelation, as He did with certain Old and New Testament saints—men like Abraham, Moses, David, Peter, John, and especially Paul. However, God has spoken to all of us through His Word, the Bible. We have at our disposal His direct revelation in written form. The Scriptures contain all we need to discover His perfect will throughout our lifetime. The question is: Are we consulting His Word regularly in order to discover His will? Furthermore, do we take advantage of the opportunity to consult Him directly through prayer as Paul exhorted us to do? (Phil. 4:6) Remember also James' exhortation: "If any of your lacks wisdom, let him ask of God, who gives to all men generously and without reproach, and it will be given to him" (James 1:5).

*Are You Wandering in "The Land of the Philistines?"*

Most Christians I know who are in trouble today are trying to scheme and engineer their way through mountains of difficulty without consulting God's will through His Word and prayer. I once knew a Christian who wandered around in "the land of the Philistines" trying to impress the world. He was out of the will of God. He got into serious trouble with the government, his business associates, his family, and his Christian friends. As long as he ignored God's will he went from bad to worse—just like David! As far as I know, he is still "wandering in the wilderness."

*Principle 3. Closely related to David's failure to consult God regarding His will was his tendency to stop trusting the Lord and to take matters into his own hands.*

When David challenged and slew Goliath, he had great confidence in God (1 Sam. 17:45). But when fear replaced his faith, he began to scheme and connive. Then he failed to do God's will. However, when he once again put his faith in God, he became successful. He could balance his human skills with the dependence upon God to use those skills to achieve the Lord's divine purposes.

This is very apparent when David emerged from the cave of Adullam and faced both the Philistine army and King Saul (chap. 23). It also was true when he came to his senses in the land of the Philistines and once again trusted God (chap. 30).

*What About You?*

How easy it is for all of us to trust in ourselves—to take matters into our own hands when we face serious challenges. I realize that this is one of my own tendencies. When I trust in myself and my own abilities, things seldom work out as they should. Careful planning and human effort are essential in solving problems, but they must be carefully balanced with trust and confidence in the Lord.

*Principle 4. David's greatest failures always followed a period of great success and popularity.*

There were three such cycles in David's life:

*Facing Goliath*

The first cycle began with David's great victory over Goliath, which led to unparalleled popularity. The theme song in Israel was that "Saul has slain his thousands, and David his ten thousands" (18:7). For a time, David could do no wrong in the eyes of Israel. He "was prospering in all his ways for the Lord was with him" (v. 14). But all this ended with a period of great failure as David attempted to escape Saul's attacks on his life with his own schemes.

*His Encounters with Saul*

David's second cycle involved his two opportunities to take Saul's life. He rose above the temptation and loved his enemy as no man in Israel had done before. Though David's witness was limited to his own relatively small band of men, this was an unusual spiritual victory. But again, this mountaintop experience descended into a valley of great failure as he traveled into the land of the Philistines seeking refuge.

*His Relationship with Bathsheba*

The third cycle of success was the longest in his life—approximately twenty years. Though not without mistakes, David lived a well-ordered and God-fearing life. As the king of Israel, he ruled his people with wisdom and righteousness. He was popular not only among his own people but also among the nations that surrounded Israel. Yet it was at this time that he committed his greatest sins—adultery and murder—which brought a period of stress and anxiety into his life that plagued him the rest of his life. Though he experienced forgiveness from God, trouble knocked at David's door until the day he died.

*What About You?*

Perhaps this is one of the greatest lessons we can learn from the overall events in David's life. We must be on constant guard during periods of great success and popularity. It's during these times that Satan can attack us—particularly on our blind side. How easy it is to be lifted up with pride and take credit and glory for ourselves. When we do, we are candidates for failure. We are tempted to stop consulting God. We take matters into our own hands. We stop trusting God and put our faith in ourselves.

## *Principle 5. At times, David misinterpreted his success and popularity as a sign of God's blanket approval on all he was doing.*

David's sojourn into the land of the Philistines is a classic illustration of this false thinking. Though he was living directly out of God's will in many ways, he still prospered. How easy it was to misinterpret and misconstrue such events as God's blessings.

### *God Does Bless Us when We're Faithful*

After David became king of all Israel, he "became greater and greater, for the LORD God of hosts was with him" (2 Sam. 5:10). This statement is almost haunting in its implications.

Here David's greatness is measured by his success as king, his popularity with the people of Israel, and his victories over his enemies. This was indeed a blessing from God! But David didn't realize that rising to popularity and success in this life is not necessarily a measurement of spiritual maturity—even though God may be adding the blessing. In fact, part of David's greatness in the eyes of the world was the number of concubines and wives he added to his harem—a direct violation of God's commands (2 Sam. 5:13; Deut. 17:17).

### *It's Possible to Move in Two Directions at the Same Time*

When David finally became king, he experienced unprecedented greatness in the eyes of men. His success in many respects was a direct blessing from God. However, at the same time David experienced deterioration in his spiritual sensitivities, which had so characterized him as a young man in love with his Creator. When David left his father's flocks and experienced a great victory over Goliath, he reached his spiritual peak. From that time forward, he experienced ups and downs. Sadly, he never reached the same level of spirituality he had experienced in his early years.

### *What About You?*

Is this kind of spiritual experience inevitable—especially as we get older? Not at all! David's life could have been a series of mountaintop experiences with the Lord. Obviously, he would need to pass through various valleys in order to climb to higher levels, but he didn't have to slide off the other side of the mountain.

### *Popularity Can Be a Curse*

Our natural tendency—like David's—is to interpret success and popularity as God's blanket approval on what we're doing. Not so! We must remember that God's grace is poured out on *all men.* No matter what our relationship with the Lord, He often continues to bless us materially and socially. If we're not careful, our spiritual lives in the eyes of the Lord may be deteriorating while our "greatness" in the eyes of men is increasing.

How tragic when this happened to David! And how tragic when it happens to us! In some instances, it also leads to a terrible catastrophe—a "Bathsheba," dishonesty, a broken family, children who turn against God.

### *Christian Leader—Be on Guard*

I know Christian leaders—don't you?—who are climbing the ladder of success and popularity. Yet it's apparent that they've lost the warmth toward God and people they once had when they began their ministerial journey. With popularity has come professionalism, spiritual pride, and a spirit of competition. In some instances these leaders have passed off the scene and are living fruitless and carnal lives. They've even lost credibility with their own family members.

This need not happen. The Word of God says that "no

temptation has overtaken you but such as is common to man; and God is faithful, who will not allow you to be tempted beyond what you are able, but with the temptation will provide the way of escape also, that you may be able to endure it" (1 Cor. 10:13).

### *Principle 6. David's greatest sins—adultery and murder—largely disqualified him from correcting and disciplining his own children when they committed the same sins.*

What could David say when his son Amnon raped his own sister Tamar? What right did he have to deal with his son Absalom when he in turn murdered Amnon for raping his sister?

It's true that he still had the responsibility to discipline his children even though he had committed sins just as flagrant as theirs. But how could he do so with a sense of freedom? Emotionally he was thwarted. The finger of ridicule and condemnation pointed at him from all directions. His conscience would condemn him, for he would feel that he didn't have a right to deal with his children and their sins when he—the king of Israel and "a man of God"—had committed the same crimes!

David never overcame this problem. His loss of self-respect and respect from others was too great. The emotional damage in his own heart was too deep to be completely healed. Forgiven? Yes! Totally exonerated in the eyes of the people? No! He bore the stigma until he died.

#### *What About You?*

There are Christians today who—like David—have emotionally and socially disqualified themselves from disciplining their own children. They have destroyed their credibility. Their words of admonition ring hollow. "Do what I say not what I do" is their only recourse. Response from those who listen comes either in "muffled words" or in "flagrant rebellion." The thought is always the same: "Hypocrite! What right have you to tell me what I can or cannot do, what is best for me, when you are as guilty as I am?"

Fortunately, most of us have not blown it nearly so badly as David. And in most instances, our children are very understanding and forgiving when they see true repentance on our part. But there is a point beyond which we cannot go without serious repercussions. David passed that point—in a sense, the point of no return—when it came to regaining respect from his own children.

### *This Need Not Happen to You*

If David were here, he would encourage us not to let this happen to us. It *need not* happen to us! For the great majority of Christian parents, there is a very bright future. But we must be on guard!

One of our great advantages is the example of David—who made such a great beginning but in many respects ended his life with a dark cloud hanging over what could have been a consistently brilliant career and walk with God. You see, all of these things are recorded for us that we might avoid David's mistakes. The question we all face however is: How willing am I to listen and to learn?

### *Principle 7. Each time David acknowledged his sin and truly repented, God forgave and restored him to fellowship with Himself.*

Though David seriously walked out of God's will on several occasions, he always turned back to the Lord with great remorse and sorrow, seeking God's forgiveness. This is why he was called a man after God's own heart. Though at times he certainly could not be characterized as this kind of man, the fact remains that he always had a sensitive and responsive heart toward God, which caused him to respond in repentance. David's gravestone could legitimately have carried the epitaph: "Here lies David, a man after God's heart (often, but not always)!"

### *An Amazing Heritage*

In the New Testament, David is most frequently mentioned in conjunction with the lineage of Jesus Christ. Our Lord and Savior is often called the Son of David. In fact, His direct line can be traced from David's offspring through Bathsheba! (Matt. 1:6)

### *What Does All of This Mean?*

Jesus Christ identified with the failures of those who walked with Him during His life on earth. However, He also identifies with the failures of mankind throughout history. This is why we read, "We have one who has been tempted in every way, just as we are—yet was without sin" (Heb. 4:15, NIV).

At the human level—something we will spend eternity attempting to understand—Jesus Christ identified with our sins without sinning. Because this is true, He understands our temptations. He is our great high priest who is able to "sympathize with our weaknesses" (Heb. 4:15). Were He not this kind of Savior, no man could be saved—including His great . . . great . . . grandfather, David.

### *What About You?*

Have you accepted Jesus Christ as your Savior from sin? Have you confessed your sins and experienced the cleansing power of His shed blood? If not, would you do that today? Simply in your own words invite Jesus Christ to be your Lord and Savior.

As a Christian, perhaps you are living out of God's will. Like David, you've blown it. If you have, acknowledge your sin, just as David did. Repent and turn back to God. Remember that "if we confess our sins, he is faithful and just and will forgive us our sins and purify us from all unrighteousness" (1 John 1:9, NIV). If God extended His mercy to a repentant heart in the Old Testament, won't He do that for you? Turn back to God now before it's too late to experience the earthly benefits of that forgiveness.

## Becoming a Man after God's Heart

As you come to the close of this study, a final exercise will give you an opportunity to take a look at David's life as a whole and what you can learn in order to be a man after God's heart. As you read the following questions, check yourself. Circle those you need to give close attention. Then select the one you believe is the most urgent. Then set a goal. For example, you may sense that you are allowing attitudes and actions to creep into your life that eventually will cause you to lose credibility with those you love the most.

____ 1. To what extent am I as a dedicated Christian assuming that my present heart attitude toward God will automatically continue throughout my lifetime?

____ 2. To what extent do I consult God through His Word and in prayer while setting my daily goals?

____ 3. To what extent do I tend to stop trusting God and take matters into my own hands?

____ 4. To what extent am I on guard against spiritual pride and an overconfident attitude when I am experiencing a period of great success in my life?

____ 5. To what extent do I interpret my successes in life and my popularity as a sign of God's approval on all that I am doing?

____ 6. To what extent am I allowing attitudes and actions to creep into my life that will eventually cause me to lose credibility with those I love the most?

____ 7. To what extent am I availing myself of the resources in Jesus Christ to forgive my sins and then to turn from those sins?

*Set a Goal*

With God's help, I will begin immediately to carry out the following goal in my life:

______________________________________________

______________________________________________

______________________________________________

______________________________________________

## *Memorize the Following Scripture*

> *Now these things happened to them as an example, and they were written for our instruction, upon whom the ends of the ages have come. Therefore let him who thinks he stands take heed lest he fall. No temptation has overtaken you but such as is common to man; and God is faithful, who will not allow you to be tempted beyond what you are able, but with the temptation will provide the way of escape also, that you may be able to endure it.*
>
> 1 CORINTHIANS 10:11–13

## *A Final Word*

If you are a young person with a lifetime before you, or if you're an older Christian who has walked with God since being a Christian, remember: We need not follow in David's footsteps when it comes to his failures. Thank God we can learn from David's experiences. That's the desire of my heart. I hope and trust it's yours.

# *Endnotes*

**Chapter 1**

1. See *The Measure of a Man,* a book based upon the qualities for spiritual leadership outlined by Paul in 1 Timothy 3 and Titus 1. This book is published by Regal Books and also written by Gene Getz.

**Chapter 2**

1. For a list of Scriptures to verify the functions of the heart, see Charles F. Pfeiffer et al., eds., *Wycliffe Bible Encyclopedia* (Chicago: Moody Press, 1975), vol. 1, 767, 768.

2. It is commonly accepted that David wrote seventy-three psalms. We cannot demonstrate this conclusively and absolutely. However, both tradition and internal evidence strongly indicate he is the authentic author.

**Chapter 3**

1. There's an interesting correlation between believers who were especially gifted by the Spirit in the Old Testament and those gifted by the Spirit in the New Testament. For example, the Corinthians were the most spiritually gifted church, yet they were the most carnal church. But their carnality did not cause God to take away their special gifts. For a time, God even allowed them to use His gifts to promote their own selfish ambitions.

**Chapter 7**

1. Alan Redpath, *The Making of a Man of God* (Westwood, N.J.: Fleming H. Revell, 1951), 61.

2. We're told in 1 Samuel 15:35 that "Samuel did not see Saul again until the day of his death;" and also that "Samuel grieved over Saul." Later, in 1 Samuel 16:2, we are told that Samuel was so fearful of Saul that he thought the king might kill him. Evidently this was Samuel's feeling until the day he died. It stands to reason then that Samuel probably offered David very little encouragement and help.

**Chapter 12**

1. David was thirty years old when he became king of Judah. He reigned seven-and-one-half years in Judah and thirty-three years over all Israel. (2 Sam. 5:4–5).